# Great Chicago Cub Baseball Players Since 1876

Gary Koca

To Bill:
Hope you enjoy the book!
Gary Koca
12/25/16
Go Cubs!!

ISBN-10:1511747455
ISBN-13:978-1511747455

# DEDICATION

This book is dedicated to my grandfather and father, two great Chicago Cub fans who instilled in me my love of baseball and the Chicago Cubs. (Some would call it a curse). My grandfather was nine when the Cubs last won a World Series in 1908, and my father never lived to see them win a World Series.

# CONTENTS

# FORWARD

Yes, Mr. Ripley, believe it or not, there were at least 25 great baseball players in the history of the Chicago Cubs!

The Chicago Cubs are undoubtedly one of major league baseball's most storied and historic franchises. Despite their complete lack of success since last appearing in a World Series in 1945, they remain one of baseball's most popular teams, with millions of fans throughout the United States and all over the world. The Cubs are one of baseball's longest continually running major league baseball teams, tracing their origins to the beginning of the National League in 1876. While the National Association – founded in 1871 – included the Boston (Atlanta) Braves, both teams have been in existence since the official beginning of the National League in 1876. However, the Cubs are the longest continually-running franchise in the same city in the history of baseball, since the Braves have played in Boston, Milwaukee, and Atlanta.

Despite the team's overall lack of success since 1945, the Chicago Cubs have fielded some of the best baseball players in the history of major league baseball. Players like A.G. Spalding, Cap Anson, Mordecai Brown, and Tinker to Evers to Chance are featured in this book along with the more recent Cub greats that include Ernie Banks, Billy Williams, Ron Santo, and Ryne Sandberg. This book will cover those specific players rather than the team as a whole, focusing of course on their years as a member of the Chicago Cubs.

A number of outstanding players have been excluded to keep the number at a manageable 25. I have excluded players whose major achievements were with other teams, including Greg Maddux, Rogers Hornsby, Grover Cleveland Alexander, Andre Dawson, and Bruce Sutter, to name a few.

# 1 BRIEF HISTORY OF THE CHICAGO CUBS

In 1871, the National Association of Professional Base Ball Players was established as baseball's first "major league." Five years later, in 1876, Chicago businessman William Hulbert formed the National League of Professional Baseball Clubs to replace the National Association, which he believed was mismanaged and corrupt. The National League had eight original members: the Boston Red Stockings (now the Atlanta Braves), Chicago White Stockings (now the Chicago Cubs), Cincinnati Red Stockings, Hartford Dark Blues, Louisville Grays, Mutual of New York, Philadelphia Athletics and the St. Louis Brown Stockings.

In 1876, the Chicago White Stockings – predecessor of the Chicago Cubs - become one of eight charter members of the National League, led by league president William A. Hulbert, who was also the owner of the Chicago team. The first game in the history of the Chicago National League Ball Club was played on April 25, 1876, with A.G. Spalding as the manager. Spalding doubled as the pitcher and recorded the first NL shutout, a 4-0 win over Louisville. The first run in team history was scored by center fielder Paul Hines on a throwing error in the second inning – now there's a trivia question for you! Who scored the first-ever Cubs run? The White Stockings went on to win the inaugural National League Championship with a 52-14 record. There was no World Series in those days, so the White Stockings, with the best record in the league, were champions.

In 1882, Hulbert died suddenly, and Al Spalding, who had retired a few years earlier to start Spalding sporting goods, assumed ownership of the club, with Adrian (Cap) Anson serving as first baseman and manager. The White Stockings proved to be the premier team in the early years of the National League. They won championships in 1876, 1880, 1881, 1882, 1885, and 1886 – six of the first 11 years of the fledging league. Led by such top-flight players as pitchers Larry Corcoran, John Clarkson, and Fred Goldsmith, infielders Cap Anson and Tom Burns, outfielders George Gore and Abner Dalrymple, and catcher Silver Flint, the White Stockings were the New York Yankees of their day. No Chicago Cub team – not even those early 1900's teams that featured Three Finger Brown, Ed Reulbach, and Tinker to

Evers to Chance - has ever approached that type of success in almost 140 years.

As player/manager, Anson established himself as the game's first true superstar and perhaps the best overall baseball player of the 19th century. Anson was the first player in history credited with collecting 3,000 career hits. He was voted by *Sporting Life* magazine as the third baseman of the decade (1870's) and as the first baseman of the decade (1880's). Unfortunately, his reputation as a player has been tarnished by his racist actions in keeping one of the first black players in professional baseball – Moses Fleetwood Walker – from having a long career in professional baseball. More on that later.

After 1886, things changed for the White Stockings. Players got older, retired, or were sent packing to other teams; the nucleus of the dominant teams of the past decade was gone, except for Anson. Following Chicago's great run during the 1880s, the on-field fortunes of Anson's team – now nicknamed the Colts - dwindled during the mid-1890s, despite the emergence of centerfielder Bill Lange, who set the club record for steals with 84 in 1897, and was one of the league's best hitters and outfielders for seven seasons. The team would have to await revival under new leadership, however, because after the 1897 season, team owner Al Spalding opted not to renew Anson's contract, and a year later Lange retired to become a real estate/insurance professional.

Baseball's popularity in general faded somewhat during the 1890s. In an apparent effort to boost attendance, in 1891 the Colts began splitting their schedule between West Side Park and the recently built South Side Park. In 1892 they played their entire schedule on the south side, but decided to move more toward the city center again. Early in the 1893 season they opened "West Side Park II", a wooden structure that would be their home for the next 23 seasons until they moved into Wrigley Field in 1916.

Anson's departure led to the team's nickname transitioning through the next few seasons. With the loss of their "Pop" as Anson had become known, at times the media referred to the club as the Colts, Remnants or most often - the Orphans. Those names remained in circulation through the 1905 season, depending on which newspaper one read. The name "Cubs" first appeared in print in 1902 - The first mention in print of "Cubs" was in the March 27, 1902, issue of the *Chicago Daily News*[1] and gained popularity over the next four years, before becoming the sole nickname in 1906. The old name, Chicago White Stockings, was adopted in 1900 by the new American Baseball League entry on Chicago's south side, initially as a minor league entry. The AL turned major in 1901, and the southsiders' adopted nickname was soon shortened by the press to Chicago White Sox.

The young talent assembled by the Cubs began to assert itself in the early 1900's. The 1903 team was on its way, featuring players like Jack Taylor, Carl Lundgren, Frank Chance, Joe Tinker, Johnny Evers, outfielder Frank Schulte, and catcher Johnny Kling. The dominant pitching staff that included Mordecai Brown, Ed Reulbach, Jack Pfiester, and Orvie Overall arrived soon after. This nucleus of players led the Cubs to three straight National League titles, a 116-36 record in 1906 (highest single season winning percentage in major league baseball history), and world championships in 1907 and 1908. The team won one more national league title in 1910 before the inevitable decline began the next year.

1908 World Champion Cubs. Last Cub championship team

---

[1] www.jackbales.com

The 1910's and 1920's were generally lean years for the Chicago National League baseball club. While they generally ended up in the first division, their only world series appearance during the 1910 decade was in 1918, where they lost to the Boston Red Sox and a pitcher – yes, pitcher – by the name of Babe Ruth. Perhaps their best player during that decade was pitcher James (Hippo) Vaughn. Not sure why he was nicknamed Hippo, other than he was 6 feet 4 inches tall and weighed at least 215 pounds. Big, but not a hippo.

The other crowning achievement of the decade of the 1910's was the opening of Wrigley Field. Originally known as Weeghman Park, Wrigley Field was built on the grounds once occupied by a seminary. Weeghman Park was originally the home of Chicago's entry into the ill-fated Federal League and was the property of Charles H. Weeghman. The team was known as the Federals and the Whales and had a very short existence. The Cubs took over in 1916 and have been there ever since. By the way, the cost of building Weeghman Park, which had a seating capacity of 14,000, was estimated at $250,000. The infield and outfield consisted of more than 4,000 yards of soil and four acres of Kentucky bluegrass. [2]

The early 1920's brought mediocrity and a series of second division finishes, but the Cub fortunes started picking up again after 1925. The team also had its first million attendance figure in 1927, drawing 1,159,168 fans. From 1929 through 1938, the Cubs won the National League pennant every three years – 1929, 1932, 1935, and 1938 – but (alas!) again no World Series championships. A series of really great players appeared in that decade, including position players Hack Wilson, Riggs Stephenson, Kiki Cuyler, Stan Hack, Billy Herman, and Billy Jurges, catcher Gabby Hartnett, and pitchers that included Charlie Root, Larry French, Lon Warneke, Guy Bush, Bill Lee, and Pat Malone.[3] The World Series of 1932 featured Babe Ruth's so-

---

[2] Chicago Cubs website

[3] Hall of Famer Rogers Hornsby had one great year with the Cubs – 1929 – but his best years were with the Cubs' greatest rival, the St. Louis Cardinals.

called called shot off Cub pitcher Charlie Root, but whether or not he called the shot, was merely tipping his cap to the fans, or engaging in some other maneuver is a story that has been debated for decades.

After 1938, things got pretty rough for the Cubs. While they did win the pennant in 1945, it was somewhat tainted because most of the best players were off fighting in World War II. The Cubs and Tigers had the best of the remaining players, and the Cubs fell to the Tigers in the World Series of 1945 in seven games. After that, it was a succession of really bad teams throughout the latter 40's, all of the 50's, and most of the 60's. Whether it was owner P.K. Wrigley being really frugal, the curse of the Billy Goat, bad luck, poor management, or refusal to play night games, the Cubs were clearly one of the doormats of the National League during that period. In the 20 years between 1947 and 1966, the Cubs finished above .500 exactly one time, and that was with a record of 82-80.

In spite of that record, some very good players and one great player wore the Cubbie blue. The year 1953 brought Ernie Banks to the Cubs from the Kansas City Monarchs of the Negro League; Banks and Gene Baker were the first African-American players on the Cubs, and Banks is arguably the greatest Cub player of all time – at least I think so. In 1959, for example, the Cubs finished 5th out of eight teams, and likely avoided the cellar only because of Banks' .304 average, 45 home runs, and 143 runs batted in.

In the late 50's and early 60's, the Cubs added additional talent like Billy Williams, Ron Santo, Fergie Jenkins, Ken Holtzman, Bill Hands, Don Kessinger, Glen Beckert, and Randy Hundley, which allowed them to remain in first place for most of the 1969 season before they collapsed while the New York Mets surged and won the National League pennant and the World Series that year. While the Cubs made the playoffs in 1984, 1989, 1998, 2003, 2007, and 2008, there was never really any sustained success, and the National League pennant and World Series appearances still eluded them. They probably should have at least appeared in the World Series in three of those years – 1984, 2003, and 2008, but for whatever reason – see the above list – they never quite made it, even when they had superior teams to the teams they lost to. 1984 and 2003 were particularly bitter endings, when a World Series appearance was clearly within reach. Even then, the Cubs were blessed with quality players like Ryne Sandberg, Mark Grace, Rick Sutcliffe, and a young Greg Maddux.[4] But still no championships.

**Statue of Mr. Cub, Ernie Banks, in front of the sign on Clark Street.**

Ownership also changed during this period of time. The Tribune Company, which includes the *Chicago Tribune* and WGN Radio and Television, bought the team from the Wrigley Company in 1981. They in turn sold the team to businessman Sam Zell in 2007, a terrible move for Cub fans by the way. Cub fans were rescued when the current owner – Tom Ricketts – a die-hard Cub fan and an extremely successful investment banker – purchased the team in 2008. With the hiring of Theo Epstein as team president and Jed Hoyer as general manager, it appears that the fortunes of the Chicago Cubs may again be on the rise, and the notion of sustained success may no longer be just a dream.

---

[4] Because of the corked bat incident and steroids issue, I have purposely failed to include Sammy Sosa in this group.

# 2 ALBERT G. SPALDING

Is it possible that the man who owned the company that manufactures and sells equipment for baseball, basketball, football, and many other sports once played for, managed, and owned the Chicago Cubs? It is, and that man is Albert G. Spalding, the owner of Spalding Sporting Goods. As good of a baseball player as he was, he was even a better businessman.

Albert G. Spalding was actually the first great Chicago Cubs player. Although he only played for the team for one year, he also served as manager and later owner for many seasons. Spalding was also an outstanding entrepreneur and businessman and co-founder of the sporting goods company that still bears his name and provides sporting goods and equipment for a number of professional sports leagues. A true success story!

But before there was a National League and before there was a team called the Chicago White Stockings, Albert Goodwin Spalding pitched for the National Association of Professional Base Ball Players from 1871 to 1875.

## Early Life and Career as a Baseball Player

Albert Goodwin Spalding was born in Byron, Illinois – a town about 75 miles west of Chicago which is now most famous for being the home of a nuclear power plant – on September 2, 1850. Spalding started playing baseball for a junior team in Rockford, Illinois from 1863 to 1866. He played first base and then became a pitcher and in 1866 he pitched for the Forest City Club of Rockford. He helped defeat the powerful Nationals of Washington, 29-23, during the team's 1867 Midwest tour in which they would finish the trip at 9-1. In that game, Spalding would only allow the Nationals to score more than five runs once and shut them out in three different innings, a remarkable achievement at that time. Spalding was then hired by the Chicago Excelsiors team for the beginning of the 1868 season and was also given a $40 per week job as a grocery store clerk.

Baseball pioneer Harry Wright brought Spalding, at a salary of about $2,000, and Ross Barnes, Spalding's shortstop on the 1867 Forest City Club, to Boston to play for the Boston Red Stockings during the inaugural season of the National Association of Professional Base Ball Players in 1871. Spalding would lead the league in wins with 19 at the age of 21, but Boston would finish second to a solid Philadelphia Athletics club.

In the winter of 1873, after only having played three years of truly professional baseball, Harry Wright selected his star 23 year-old pitcher, Albert Spalding, to sail to England and to garner interest for a baseball tour featuring the Boston Red Stockings and the Philadelphia Athletics. While the tour did little to raise interest in baseball in England and was not a financial success, it demonstrates how well regarded Spalding was at the time.

For the final four seasons of the NA, Spalding would lead the league in wins and the Red Stockings would finish first. In 1875, Boston would finish 71-8 and Spalding would achieve a career high 54 wins.

During that season he also had personal winning streaks of 22 and 24 games.

Throughout the National Association's five year existence, Albert Spalding was clearly its best pitcher. He was the first professional pitcher to win 50, 100, 150 and 200 games and finished with a 207-56 record in the National Association.

At some point in the National Association's final season in 1875, William Hulbert approached Spalding and asked him to play for him in a newly forming league. Even though Spalding was still under contract with the Red Stockings, Hulbert, who was the President of the Chicago White Stockings and soon to be founder of the National League of Professional Base Ball Clubs, convinced Spalding to leave Boston at the end of the season, basically to return to his home town. Hulbert offered Spalding $4000 and a quarter of the gate receipts to be the pitcher, captain and manager of the White Stockings. Once Spalding agreed to the contract, Hulbert used Albert's influence to help recruit three other Red Stocking players and then took him to Philadelphia to sign another outstanding player, Adrian (Cap) Anson.

In 1876, Spalding won 47 games as the primary pitcher for the White Stockings and led them to win the first-ever National League pennant by a wide margin. (Spalding won 47 of the team's 52 wins that year, and started most of the games.) Also in 1876, Albert Spalding, along with his brother Walter and with an $800 advance, opened a small athletic equipment store in Chicago. He became the first professional pitcher to win 250 career games that year.

In 1877, Spalding began to use a glove to protect his catching hand. People had used gloves previously, but never had a star like Spalding used one. Spalding had an ulterior motive for doing so: his sporting goods store sold baseball gloves, and wearing one himself was good advertising for his business. Shrewd move!

Spalding retired from playing baseball in 1878 at the age of 27, although he continued as president and part owner of the White Stockings and a major influence on the National League. Spalding's .796 career winning percentage (from an era when teams played about once or twice a week) is the highest ever achieved by a baseball pitcher.

**Spalding's Business Career after Baseball**

Unlike many of the players of the time, Albert Spalding had a shrewd business sense and capitalized on that by combining baseball with business for an extremely lucrative career for the 40 years after his playing days were over.

**Albert Spalding, baseball executive and businessman**

Spalding became the White Stockings secretary and Hulbert's right hand man in 1878. Not surprisingly, being a good businessman, his baseball became the official ball used by the National League in 1878, and he supplied the NL with free baseballs and gave them one dollar for each dozen that they used.[5] In 1878 he also published the first

---

[5] www.19cbaseball.com

official Spalding's Base Ball Guide. He employed Henry Chadwick, who was the premier baseball writer and carried the title of "Father of the Game," to edit his annual guide. The Spalding Sporting Goods Company paid the National League a fee for exclusive publishing rights. In 1879, the ever-resourceful Spalding opened a bat factory.

During the 1880's, he bought out many of his competitors but continued to sell sporting goods under their original brand names to give the illusion of competition. Spalding was reportedly selling a million bats per year by 1887. Starting in 1899, A. G. Spalding & Bros. allowed other retailers to order directly from their catalog. In 1891, Spalding had ten large factories located in different parts of the United States, where they manufactured vast quantities of athletic goods such as uniforms and clothing for sports' wear, baseballs, tennis balls, athletic suits of all kinds, bicycles, boats, fishing tackles, athletic shoes, and an endless variety of gymnasium outfits.

Spalding employed more than 3,500 people by 1896, and had plants scattered across the eastern half of America. Spalding eventually bought Wright & Ditson, a sporting goods manufacturer out of Boston and the maker of the rival Players' League Official Base Ball; A.J. Reach, a sporting goods company out of Philadelphia and the maker of the official baseball for the American Association (another rival league of the National League); and Peck & Snyder, a popular sporting goods manufacturer out of New York.

Also, after William Hulbert's death in April 1882, Spalding became the owner and President of the Chicago White Stockings at the age of 31. In April of 1891, he stepped down from being president of the team. During his tenure in Chicago's front office, his teams never finished below .500, finished first five times, second four times, third twice and fourth three times. His White Stockings tied the St. Louis Browns 3-3-1 in the 1885 "World's Series"[6] and lost the 1886 World's Series to St. Louis, 4-2. However, they were clearly the New York

---

[6] The official World Series did not begin until 1903 between the National and American Leagues. This was just an unofficial battle between rival leagues. Rumor has it that the White Stockings did not take it all that seriously.

Yankees of their day. In 1892, the first year without Spalding's direct involvement, Chicago finished in seventh place and under .500. Spalding sold the club in 1902.

As a baseball executive, Spalding did not care much for the typical player. He felt that their excessive drinking, gambling and overall bad behavior hurt the game. He wanted clean, upstanding players to promote and mold the game. Being a very successful businessman, Spalding had little tolerance for the bad habits he saw among many of the players.

For example, after losing the 1886 "World's Series" to the American Association's St. Louis Browns, Spalding sold his star player, Mike "King" Kelly, to the Boston Beaneaters for the-then monumental sum of $10,000. The 1886 NL batting champion was reviled by Spalding for his life style and constant high maintenance. He also shipped centerfielder George Gore to the New York Giants. After the 1887 season Spalding shipped John Clarkson, the NL's top pitcher, again to the Beaneaters, also for $10,000. The cantankerous owner disliked the high-strung pitcher and did not want to have his manager Cap Anson's ego compete with Clarkson's. But there were consequences: These were really good players who were getting traded. As a result, at the end of the 1889 season both the New York Giants and the Boston Beaneaters finished ahead of the third place White Stockings.

In 1888–1889, Spalding took a group of major league players around the world to promote baseball and, by the way, also Spalding sporting goods. This was the first-ever world baseball tour. Playing across the western U.S.,[7] the tour also made stops in Hawaii, New Zealand, Australia, Ceylon, Egypt, Italy, France, and England. The tour returned to grand receptions in New York, Philadelphia, and Chicago and included future Hall of Famers Cap Anson and John Montgomery Ward. While the players were on the tour, the National League instituted new rules regarding player pay that led to a revolt of players, led by Ward, who started the Players League the following

---

[7] Remember, there were no teams west of St. Louis at the time.

season (1890). The league lasted one year, partially due to the anti-competitive tactics of Spalding to limit its success. As I said, Spalding was no fool when it came to astute business practices that benefitted his pocketbook.

## Later Life

In 1900, Spalding moved to San Diego with his second wife, Elizabeth, and became a prominent member and supporter of the Theosophical community Lomaland, which was being developed on Point Loma by Katherine Tingley.[8] He built an estate in the Sunset Cliffs area of Point Loma where he lived with Elizabeth for the rest of his life. They raised race horses and collected Chinese fine furniture and art. (I'm sure King Kelly never collected fine Chinese art, although he may have eaten Chinese food once in a while.)

The Spaldings had an extensive library which included many volumes on Theosophy, art, and literature. In 1907-1909 he was the driving force behind the development of a paved road, known as the "Point Loma boulevard," from downtown San Diego to Point Loma and Ocean Beach; the road also provided good access to Lomaland. It later provided the basis for California State Route 209. He proposed the project, supervised it on behalf of the city, and paid a portion of the cost out of his own pocket. He joined with other civic-minded businessmen to purchase the site of the original Presidio of San Diego, which they developed as a historic park and eventually donated to the city of San Diego. Spalding also ran unsuccessfully for the United States Senate in 1910. He helped to organize the 1915 Panama-California Exposition, serving as second vice-president.

Albert Goodwin Spalding died on September 9, 1915 at the age of 65 in San Diego, and his ashes were scattered at his request. He had a profound impact on the development of baseball in general and the Chicago Cubs in particular during the last quarter of the 19th century.

---

[8] The goal of theosophy is to explore the origin of divinity and humanity, and the world. From investigation of those topics, theosophists try to discover a coherent description of the purpose and origin of the universe.

# 3 ADRIAN (CAP) ANSON

If people have heard of any one single Chicago Cub baseball player before 1900, it would probably be Adrian Anson.

Adrian (Cap) Anson, baseball's first superstar, was the dominant on-field figure of nineteenth-century baseball and a Chicago Cub for just about all of that time.[9] He was a small-town kid from Iowa who earned his fame as the player/manager of the fabled Chicago White Stockings, now of course the Cubs as I have said several times already. A larger-than-life figure of great talents and great faults, Anson managed the White Stockings to five pennants and set all the batting records that players such as Ty Cobb and Babe Ruth later broke. Anson was the second manager (after Harry Wright) to win

---

[9] Anson did play for the National Association from 1871-1875 before joining the White Stockings.

1,000 games and the first player to stroke 3,000 hits (though his exact total varies from one source to another). Although he retired from active play in 1897, he is still the all-time leader in hits, runs scored, doubles, and runs batted in for the Chicago franchise. Not even Ernie Banks can top his numbers in those categories. And they did not play as many games per season then.[10]

Adrian Constantine Anson, named after two towns in southern Michigan that his father admired, was born in a log cabin in Marshall (later Marshalltown), Iowa, on April 17, 1852. Adrian was the third son of Henry and Jeannette Rice Anson, and was the first pioneer child born in the town that his father had founded. Adrian, whose family proudly claimed descent from the British naval hero Lord Anson, was a big, strapping boy and possessed a self-admitted aversion to schoolwork and chores. Not until his teenage years, when baseball fever swept through Marshalltown, did Adrian find an acceptable outlet for his energy and enthusiasm. He practiced diligently and earned a place on the town team, the Marshalltown Stars, at the age of 15. The Stars, with Henry Anson at third base, Adrian's brother Sturgis in center field, and Adrian at second base, won the Iowa state championship in 1868. (Was Sturgis named after a town in Wisconsin?)

Henry Anson enrolled his sons in a preparatory course at the College of Notre Dame for two years beginning in 1865, but Adrian was more interested in baseball and skating than in his studies. A later enrollment at the state college in Iowa City (now the University of Iowa) ended similarly. Young Adrian Anson wanted to play professional baseball, and his break came in 1870 when the famous Rockford Forest City club and its star pitcher, Al Spalding, came to Marshalltown for a pair of games. The Forest City team won both matches, but the Anson family played so impressively that the Rockford management sent contract offers to all three of the Ansons. Henry and Sturgis turned Rockford down, but Adrian accepted and joined the Forest City squad in the spring of 1871.

---

[10] Teams generally played 130-140 games per season in those days.

The 19-year-old Adrian, dubbed "The Marshalltown Infant," batted .325 for Rockford and established himself as one of the stars of the new National Association. The last-place Rockford team disbanded at season's end, but the pennant-winning Philadelphia Athletics quickly signed Adrian to a contract. He rewarded the Athletics with a .415 average in 1872, third best in the Association. Anson played third base for the Athletics that season, but spent the next three seasons shuttling from first to third base with occasional stops at second, shortstop, catcher, and the outfield. (First base and third base would become his most typical positions with the White Stockings.) He also quickly became one of Philadelphia's most popular players.

Boston Red Stockings manager Harry Wright had always dreamed of introducing baseball to England, his home country, and in 1874 Wright and his star pitcher Al Spalding organized a mid-season trip to England. The Red Stockings and the Philadelphia Athletics took a three-week break from National Association play and sailed to England, where they played both baseball and cricket for British crowds. Adrian Anson led all the players on both teams in batting during the tour, and, more importantly, began a friendship with Spalding. Both were young men from the Midwest, less than two years apart in age, and both had chosen baseball over other career possibilities. Each found reasons to admire the other, and their relationship would play an important role in Anson's life for the next 30 years.

## Career with the White Stockings

During the 1875 season, Chicago club president William Hulbert signed four of Boston's brightest stars, including pitcher Al Spalding, to play for his White Stockings in the new National League in 1876. Spalding recommended that Hulbert also sign two Philadelphia standouts, Ezra Sutton and Adrian Anson. Sutton and Anson reached agreements with Hulbert, though Sutton later reneged on his deal and returned to the Athletics. Anson moved to Chicago in early 1876, and the White Stockings, managed by Spalding (who also pitched most of the games) and powered by Anson and batting champ Ross Barnes, won the first National League pennant that year.

At the same time, Anson began dating Virginia Fiegal, daughter of a saloon owner, during his Philadelphia days. He met Virginia when he was 20 and she only 13 or 14, though this was not considered unusual at the time. Their relationship hit a roadblock after Adrian signed his contract with Chicago, when Virginia strongly objected to Adrian's desire to leave Philadelphia. Anson was no contract-jumper, so he offered William Hulbert $1,000 to buy his way out of the agreement. Hulbert refused, and Anson, unwilling to break his contract and not wanting to lose Virginia, asked Virginia's father for his daughter's hand in marriage. Adrian and Virginia were wed in November 1876 (by then she was 18) and started a family that eventually produced four daughters, all of whom grew to adulthood, and three sons who died in infancy.

Adrian Anson, powerfully built at six feet two inches and 225 pounds – think Anthony Rizzo - was the biggest and strongest man in baseball during the 1870s. Some reports state that he did not take a full swing at the plate; instead, he pushed his bat at the ball and relied upon his strong arms and wrists to produce line drives. (This would seem to make sense since, despite being the strongest player in the game, he never once led the league in home runs.) An outstanding placehitter, Anson and the White Stockings worked an early version of the hit-and-run play to perfection. So good was Anson's bat control that he struck out only once during the 1878 season and twice in 1879. (Today, some players strike out 200 or more times a season.) He also served as Spalding's assistant on the field, enthusiastically cheering his teammates and arguing with opponents and umpires. Anson had managed the Philadelphia Athletics for the last few weeks of the 1875 season, and looked forward to the day that he would succeed Spalding as leader of the White Stockings

The White Stockings failed to repeat as champions under Spalding in 1877. Spalding then moved into the club presidency, but passed over Anson and appointed Bob Ferguson as his successor. Ferguson's regime was a failure, and Spalding named Anson as captain and manager for the 1879 season. He was now "Cap" Anson, and in one of his first decisions, the former utility man planted himself at first base and remained there for the rest of his career. His 1879 team challenged for the pennant, but fell apart after Anson was sidelined due to illness in late August. However, Anson's 1880 White Stockings, fortified by newcomers such as catcher/outfielder Mike Kelly, pitcher Larry Corcoran, and outfielders George Gore and Abner Dalrymple, won the championship with a .798 winning percentage, the highest in league history.

Two more pennants followed in 1881 and 1882 as Anson, who won the batting title in 1881 with a .399 mark, cemented his stature as the hardest hitter and best manager in the game. He used his booming voice and belligerent manner to rile opponents and frighten umpires, and made himself the focus of attention in nearly every game he played. His outbursts against the intimidated umpires earned him the title "King of Kickers." The White Stockings followed Anson's lead and played a hustling, battling brand of baseball that won no friends in other league cities, but put Chicago on the top of the baseball world. As baseball grew in popularity, the handsome and highly successful Cap Anson became the sport's first true national celebrity.

**Cap Anson – without the mustache but in White Stockings uniform**

Regrettably, Anson used his stature to drive minority players from the game. An 1883 exhibition game in Toledo, Ohio, between the local team and the White Stockings nearly ended before it began when Anson angrily refused to take the field against Toledo's African-American catcher, Moses Fleetwood Walker. Faced with the loss of gate receipts, Anson relented after a loud protest, but his belligerent attitude made Anson, wittingly or not, the acknowledged leader of the segregation forces already at work in the game. Other players and managers followed Anson's lead, and similar incidents occurred with regularity for the rest of the decade. In 1887, Anson made headlines again when he refused to play an exhibition in Newark unless the local club removed its African-American battery, catcher Walker and pitcher George Stovey, from the field. Teams and leagues began to bar minorities from participation, and by the early 1890's, no black players remained in the professional ranks. (So Jackie Robinson was not really the first African-American in professional baseball. Moses Fleetwood Walker was, some 64 years earlier.)

Chicago was the highest-scoring team in baseball, and Anson, as its cleanup hitter, was the leading run producer in the game. The *Chicago Tribune* introduced a new statistic, runs batted in, in 1880 and reported that Cap Anson led the league in this category by a healthy margin. The statistic was soon dropped, but later researchers have determined that Anson led the National League in RBI's eight times. He is credited with driving in more than 2,000 runs, behind only Henry Aaron and Babe Ruth on the all-time list despite the fact that National League teams played fewer than 100 games per season for the early part of Anson's career.

Despite his size and strength, as I have previously noted, Cap Anson was not a home run hitter. In fact, Anson hit more than twelve homers in a season only once. He swatted 21 round-trippers in 1884 by taking advantage of the tiny Chicago ballpark, which featured a left field fence only 180 feet from home plate (balls hit over the fence had been ruled as doubles in previous seasons). On August 5 and 6, 1884, Anson belted five homers in two games, a record that has been tied (by Stan Musial, among others) but never broken. However,

Anson drove in most of his runs with sharp line drives that the barehanded infielders found nearly impossible to stop. Baseball gloves were common in the National League by the mid 1880s, but Anson's production continued uninterrupted. He batted .300 or better in each of his first 20 professional seasons, and by 1886 he was baseball's all-time leader in games played, runs, hits, RBI, and several other categories.

As a first baseman, he was an integral part of the celebrated "Stonewall Infield" with third baseman Tom Burns, shortstop Ed Williamson, and second baseman Fred Pfeffer. This unit remained together for seven seasons, from 1883 to 1889, and formed the backbone of the Chicago defense.

Anson had been a teetotaler since his younger days, but his White Stockings were a hard-drinking crew that offended the captain. His 1883 and 1884 teams failed to win the pennant, partially due to off-the-field controversies, but in 1885 the White Stockings reclaimed their place at the top of the league. New pitcher John Clarkson posted a 53-16 record and led the team to the pennant after a spirited race against the New York Giants. However, Anson's team played poorly in a post-season "World's Series" against the St. Louis Browns of the American Association. The series ended, officially, in a tie after a disputed Browns victory caused no end of controversy. In 1886 Anson drove in 147 runs in 125 games and led the White Stockings to the pennant once again, but his team lost the six-game "World's Series" against the Browns when some of the Chicago players appeared to be inebriated on the field.[11]

After 1886, Spalding and Anson decided to break up the team, selling Mike Kelly to Boston for a then-record $10,000 and dropping veterans George Gore and Abner Dalrymple, among others. (Gore hit .304 in 1886, while Dalrymple was clearly on the down part of his career.) The 1887 squad was a better-behaved bunch, but finished in third place despite Anson's outstanding performance at bat. The 35-year-old captain won the batting title with a career-best .421 in a year

---

[11] www.capanson.com

in which walks counted as hits (though later researchers removed the 60 walks from his hit totals, leaving his average at .347 and giving the title to Detroit's Sam Thompson). In early 1888 Spalding continued the breakup by selling John Clarkson, baseball's best pitcher (who had a 38-21 record that year), to Boston for $10,000. Several new pitchers tried, and failed, to fill Clarkson's shoes, and the White Stockings finished second despite another batting championship by Anson.

After the 1888 season Spalding, owner of the sporting goods company that still bears his name, took the Chicago club and a team of National League all-stars on a baseball excursion around the world. Virginia Anson accompanied the party as Anson directed the White Stockings in New Zealand, Australia, Ceylon, Egypt, and the European continent. The trip lost money for its backers, including Anson, but it introduced baseball (and again advertised Spalding's business) to countries that had never seen the sport before. Anson often described the six-month adventure as being the high point of his life, and it takes up nearly half of Anson's autobiography, published in 1900. At the conclusion of the trip, in April of 1889, Spalding signed Anson to an unprecedented 10-year contract as player and manager of the White Stockings.

By 1890, Anson was a stockholder in the Chicago ballclub, owning 13 percent of the team. A company man through and through, he bitterly criticized the Brotherhood of Professional Ball Players, whose members quit the National League *en masse* in early 1890 and formed the Players League. Anson, one of a handful of stars who refused to jump to the new league, hastily assembled a new group of youngsters (which the newspapers dubbed Anson's Colts) and finished second that year. Spalding worked behind the scenes to undermine the rival circuit, while Anson led the charge in the newspapers, denouncing the jumpers as "traitors" and gleefully predicting the eventual failure of the upstart league. The new circuit collapsed after one season, but Anson's role in the defeat angered many of his former players.

Some reporters called Anson "the man who saved the National League," but many former Players Leaguers hated the Chicago captain for his attitude toward them. Such stars as Hugh Duffy and

George Van Haltren refused to return to Chicago after the collapse of the rival circuit, costing Anson much-needed talent. In 1891, Anson's Colts held first place until mid-September, but an 18-game winning streak vaulted Boston into the lead amid rumors that Boston opponents threw games to keep the pennant out of Anson's hands. Chicago finished in second place, and Cap Anson believed for the rest of his life that he lost the championship through the machinations of his former Players League rivals.

Anson, after more than 20 years as a player, began to slow down. His average dipped below .300 for the first time in 1891, though he led the league once again in runs batted in with 120. He had never been a great fielder (surehanded but not very mobile), but now covered so little ground at first base that the pitcher and second baseman had to help out on balls hit to the right side. As stubborn as ever, Anson was the last bare-handed first baseman in the major leagues, finally donning a glove in 1892. At bat, Anson produced one last hurrah with a remarkable .388 average in 1894 at the age of 42, but his slowness on the base paths bogged down the Chicago offense. As a manager, his increasing strictness and inflexibility angered his players. He was baseball's biggest celebrity, even enjoying a run as an actor on Broadway in a play called "A Runaway Colt" in December of 1895, but his Colts fell steadily in the standings.

His position as manager was weakened in 1891 when Al Spalding stepped down as team president. Anson might have been willing to retire from the field and accept the position of team president, but Spalding, who retained controlling ownership in the team, appointed former Boston manager Jim Hart to the post. Anson held little regard for Hart, who had served Spalding as business manager of the round-the-world tour four years before, and the two men clashed often over personnel and disciplinary matters during the next several seasons.

Spalding and Hart reorganized the club in 1892, and Anson signed a new contract with the Chicago ballclub. This agreement retained Anson's 13 percent stake in the team, but cut one year off his previous 10-year pact, though Anson claimed that he did not discover the discrepancy until later. At any rate, the new agreement expired on February 1, 1898. Anson, who by 1894 was the oldest player in the league, stubbornly kept himself in the lineup despite his dwindling production and his deteriorating relationships with Hart and the Chicago players. He batted .285 in 1897, a respectable figure today but well below the league average, and his Colts finished in ninth place. Spalding and Hart declined to renew his contract, and after 27 seasons, Cap Anson's career was over. The 45-year-old Anson retired as baseball's all-time leader in games played, plate appearances, runs, hits, doubles, runs batted in, and wins as a manager.

## Life after the White Stockings for Anson

Spalding offered to hold a testimonial benefit for Anson and raise $50,000 as a going-away gift, but Anson proudly turned it down, explaining that accepting such an offer would "stultify my manhood" and smacked of charity. The former Chicago captain then accepted a position as manager of the New York Giants, succeeding Bill Joyce, who had been sharply criticized by the national press for his part in an ugly on-field brawl. Giants' owner Andrew Freedman promised Anson full control of the team, but continually interfered with personnel and management issues. He also ignored Anson's request to trade or release Joyce, who remained on the team and retained the allegiance of many of the players. Anson led the Giants to a 9-13 record before Freedman fired him and reinstated Joyce after the controversy over the brawl died down.

After his humiliating exit from the Giants, Anson tried to obtain a Western League franchise and move it to the South Side of Chicago (remember, this is before the Chicago White Sox), but Spalding, whose approval for the move was necessary under the rules of the National Agreement, refused permission – surprise, surprise! This act ended the decades-long friendship between the two men. Anson then served as president of a revived American Association, which attempted to begin play in 1900 but folded due to financial pressures. After this defeat, Anson expressed his bitterness in his autobiography, *A Ball Player's Career.* "Baseball as at present conducted is a gigantic monopoly," stated Anson, "intolerant of opposition, and run on a grab-all-that-there-is-in-sight basis that is alienating its friends and disgusting the very public that has so long and cheerfully given to it the support that it has withheld from other forms of amusement."

Cap Anson was finished with the National League, and although he lived for another two decades, he would never again hold any official position in organized baseball.

## Life after Baseball for Cap Anson

Instead, Anson opened a bowling and billiards emporium in downtown Chicago and served as a vice-president of the new American Bowling Congress. He captained a team that won the ABC five-man national title in 1904, making Anson one of the few men in history to win championships in more than one sport (baseball and bowling – very unusual indeed). He then turned his energies to what appeared to be a promising political career. Elected to a term as Chicago city clerk in 1905, Anson soon became embroiled in numerous controversies that he was, by personality and temperament, unable to overcome. He lost a bid for re-nomination, and his career in public service ended badly. His bowling and billiards business also floundered, and in late 1905 the cash-strapped Anson sold his remaining stock in the Chicago ballclub and severed his 29-year connection with the team. (I guess he should have taken that $50,000 going-away present!)

Anson then devoted himself to semipro ball, investing most of his remaining money in his own team (called Anson's Colts) and building his own ballpark on the South Side. This effort was a money-loser, and in desperation Anson donned a uniform in 1908 and played first base at the age of 56. He could still hit, but was nearly immobile in the field, and his Colts finished in the middle of the City League standings for three seasons. In those years, Anson played many games against the Chicago Leland Giants, the leading African-American team of the era, ironically without any apparent complaints from players on the Giants. Anson, his finances stretched to the limit, sold his team after the 1909 season and returned to the stage. He created a monologue and performed it in vaudeville houses throughout the Midwest for the next few years.

## Cap Anson on Vaudeville

Anson's later life was filled with disappointment. The National League offered to provide a pension for the ex-ballplayer, but Anson stoutly refused all offers of assistance. He declared bankruptcy in 1910, and by 1913 he had lost his home and moved in with a daughter and son-in-law. Virginia Anson died in 1915 after a long illness, and the widowed ex-ballplayer resumed his stage career in a skit written by his friend Ring Lardner titled "First Aid for Father." The skit starred Anson and his daughters Adele and Dorothy, and the Anson clan crisscrossed the nation, sharing bills with jugglers and animal acts in both small town and big cities. The Vaudeville experience permitted Anson to support himself, but barely, and he retired, penniless, from the stage in 1921. He died on April 14, 1922, three days shy of his 70th birthday, and was buried in Oak Woods Cemetery in Chicago. The National League paid his funeral expenses. Seventeen years later, on May 2, 1939, both Anson and his former friend and mentor Al Spalding were named to the Baseball Hall of Fame by a special committee, a very worthy move for two of the biggest names in 19th century baseball.

# 4 LARRY CORCORAN

I had never heard much of Larry Corcoran before I started writing this book, but he certainly is an interesting as well as tragic story.

In the 1880's, pitching in baseball was quite different than today. The distance from home plate to the pitcher's mound was 50 feet, compared to the current distance of 60 feet, 6 inches. Teams generally employed only one or two pitchers, who pitched every game or every other game. As a result, few pitchers lasted past the age of 30 – they literally could not throw anymore.

**Larry Corcoran – all 5 foot 3 and 125 pounds of him.**

A perfect example of that was Larry Corcoran. Corcoran was a terrific pitcher for the Chicago White Stockings during that era – 1880 through 1885. He was one of two pitchers the White Stockings used in most of those years; he pitched in 62 percent of the games between 1880 and 1884, and the White Stockings won championships in two of those years – 1880 and 1881. Corcoran had a record of 175-85 with the White Stockings, and an overall lifetime mark of 177-89, so just about all of his wins were with the team that would eventually be known as the Cubs. And like most pitchers of that era, he pitched so many innings that he hurt his arm and was completely out of baseball by the age of 28.

Larry Corcoran was born in August of 1859 in Brooklyn, New York. Corcoran was right handed, and threw three no-hitters throughout the course of his career, including the fourth no-hitter ever recorded. We know very little about his early career before 1880. We do know that Larry Corcoran appeared on the mound for the semi-pro Mutual and Chelsea clubs of his native Brooklyn in the early weeks of the 1877 season, transferring to the Geneseo Livingstons in late June. By August, he was a member of Buffalo pitching staff, as that city entered the ranks of professional baseball for the first time.

All these clubs, like Springfield for which he pitched in 1878 and 1879, were mediocre at best, but future stardom had already been predicted for Corcoran. "He has wonderful speed for his strength, and with it a troublesome curve. He also has more than ordinary command of the ball in delivery for so swift a pitcher. He is a good 'headwork' player in the position, and with such a catcher as Snyder or Flint able to support his great pace, it would be difficult to get a base-hit from his pitching." Those words describing Corcoran appeared in the September 13, 1879 issue of the *New York Clipper*.

The following month it was announced that Corcoran would pitch for Chicago in the 1880 season. A highlight of the 1880 campaign was Corcoran's June 4 16-inning 1-1 tie against Providence and John Montgomery Ward.

## Career with the Chicago White Stockings

Corcoran was 20 years old entering his first season of Major League Baseball with the Chicago White Stockings in 1880. The White Stockings had a great season in 1880. They went 67-17 under manager Cap Anson. That year George Gore led the team in hitting with a .360 batting average.

Despite Anson and Gore's hitting, Corcoran was the heart and soul of the ball club. In his rookie season, Corcoran went 43-14 with a 1.95 ERA. He threw a career high 536.1 innings and led the league in strikeouts with 268. He started 60 games for the White Stockings in 1880, completing 57 of them – yes, 57 complete games! Corcoran even helped out offensively in 1880; batting .231 with 11 doubles and 25 RBI in 72 games. Keep in mind, Corcoran was a 20 year old rookie accomplishing these feats in his first season of Major League Baseball.

From June 7 through July 13, he won 13 consecutive games. Corcoran's 1-hit victory on August 10 against Ward was surpassed nine days later when he held Boston hitless in a 6-0 triumph. His 43 victories that year are the third highest in baseball history for a rookie - topped only by the 1876 totals of Al Spalding (47) and George Bradley (45). Corcoran's 1881 games-won total fell to 31, but it was still good enough to tie for the National League lead with Jim Whitney of Boston. His top pitching performance of the year was on August 4, a 2-hit shutout against Buffalo and Jim Galvin. Corcoran's combined victory total of 74 for his first two years has been surpassed in baseball history only by Matt Kilroy's 75 gained for Baltimore in 1886-1887.

This was the second season of a five year stretch where Corcoran averaged 34 wins per season. Corcoran had 170 career wins by the age of 25. In 1882 for example, Corcoran enjoyed two 10-game winning streaks: June 29 through July 29 and September 1 through September 30. The latter streak included a no-hitter against Worcester on Sept. 20. Chicago's support at the plate for Corcoran was excellent; they scored six or more runs in 23 of his 40 games, including 35 runs scored on July 24.

After returning to the 30-victory circle in 1883, Corcoran for awhile considered signing with the Chicago club of the fledgling Union Association for the succeeding season. He was, however, forced to rejoin the White Stockings for a reputed $2,100 after Chicago owner Spalding threatened him with blacklisting – not bad money in those days! Corcoran's 1884 season featured his third no-hitter (on June 27 against Providence). Corcoran by then had reached the 30-victory plateau four times - a total exceeded by only five mound immortals: Kid Nichols (7), Tim Keefe (6), John Clarkson (6), Cy Young (5) and Tony Mullane (5).

At the end of the first four weeks of the 1885 season, Corcoran's won-lost record stood at 5-2. It was then reported that he had so strained the muscles of his shoulder that he couldn't throw. In the next few weeks, he showed no improvement and Chicago gave him his release – not uncommon in those early days of professional baseball.

New York signed him in July, but he took the mound only three times for the Giants, winning 2 and losing 1. His 8-3 victory over St. Louis on October 8 of 1885 was the last game he was to win in the majors, at the age of 26. Corcoran pitched only four games after 1885 - two each in 1886 and 1887 - and was charged with the loss in three of those games.

Interestingly, Corcoran was the first pitcher to work out a set of signals with his catcher. He would chew tobacco, and at the suggestion of catcher Silver Flint, he would move his chew from one side of his mouth to the other, indicating when he would throw a curve ball. He also worked as an umpire for a time in the Atlantic League after his playing career was finished. A heavy drinker, Corcoran died from Bright's Disease – chronic nephritis, a kidney disease - in 1891 at the age of 32.[12] His .663 winning percentage is eighth all-time. He was interred in the Holy Sepulchre Cemetery in East Orange. Interestingly, Larry's brother, Mike, pitched in one major league game in 1884.

Corcoran possessed all the attributes of greatness except durability. He could've been one of baseball's greatest pitchers had injuries caused by overuse not plagued his career.

---

[12] Famous victims of Bright's Disease included poet Emily Dickenson, President of the United States Chester A. Arthur, baseball player Ty Cobb, botanist Gregor Mendel, and Bram Stoker, who wrote *Dracula*.

# 5 MICHAEL (KING) KELLY

While Cap Anson was the BEST baseball player of the 19th century, Mike "King" Kelly was definitely the most popular player of that era. In fact, he was the best known American of his time.[13] He was handsome, projected charisma, and played the game with a natural flair for the dramatic. He was also the single most important reason that women became attracted to baseball. Before Kelly, baseball was considered a sport played by ruffians, and very few females could be found at baseball games. Mike "King" Kelly was truly first among American baseball legends.

To show how popular he was, Ray Milland played a pitcher named King Kelly in the 1949 baseball movie "It Happens Every Spring." This film, about a chemistry professor who invents a substance that

---

[13] http://fromdeeprightfield.com/

repels wood which leads to his decision to test its effectiveness by becoming a baseball pitcher, is certainly a tribute to the original King Kelly, even though the real King Kelly had died 50+ years earlier.

King Kelly may not have been the fastest player in history, but he was one of the greatest base runners ever. Maybe he didn't have the "flat out" speed of a Maury Wills, Ricky Henderson, or Vince Coleman, but he was fast enough, and understood game situations—and could read pitchers and catchers and infielders with alarming accuracy. Not only that, but he had the instinct to steal bases at critical junctures in games…and did it with crowd-pleasing style. He is credited with inventing the "hook" slide, a strategy that revolutionized base stealing. He would "juke" an infielder into defending a particular line to the bag, then slide to a different line in order to avoid the tag. That type of slide became a common practice for about 100 years until today's players decided to go for the head-first slide, which does nothing but cause injuries.[14] The excitement generated by his base running catapulted Mike "King" Kelly into becoming perhaps the most popular of all baseball legends.

Michael Joseph Kelly was born to Irish immigrant parents in Troy, N. Y., on New Year's Eve, 1857. After the Civil War (in which his father fought on the Northern side), Kelly's father moved the family to Paterson, N. J., for work, but became ill and died when Kelly was just 13. Kelly was a bright but indifferent student. He spent most of his time on the sandlot baseball field. He was an excellent athlete, and a player who was destined to be a star of the 1880s, and William "Blondie" Purcell – a player/manager for 12 years from Paterson, New Jersey - signed Kelly (at age 15) to his amateur traveling team. Al Spalding, the former star pitcher and, of course, head of Spalding Sporting Goods and Chicago's National League franchise, then signed Kelly to his team just prior to an off-season baseball tour of California, in 1880. Kelly played 7 years with Spalding's team—and along with Cap Anson was its principle gate attraction. He played

---

[14] I know for a fact that the Chicago White Sox have told Adam Eaton that he has to avoid the reckless, head-first slide so that he can actually play in more than 120 games per year.

some right field (he had a strong throwing arm) but mostly catcher. Kelly developed real skills in calling pitches and setting defenses.

## Career with the White Stockings

Experts believed that Kelly averaged an estimated 45% success rate in throwing out base runners on attempted steals.[15] Along the way, Kelly helped Chicago win 5 pennants, including an incredible 87-25 (.777) record in 1885, a percentage which eclipsed even the great 1906 Cub team. Mike "King" Kelly truly became the cornerstone of American baseball legends.

**The 1885 Chicago White Stockings (87-25, with a .777 winning percentage). Top Row: L-R: George Gore (LF), Silver Flint (C), Cap Anson (Mgr./1B), Sy Sutcliffe (UT), Mike 'King' Kelly (RF/C), Fred Pfeffer (2B). Bottom Row: L-R: Larry Corcoran (P), Ned Williamson (SS), Abner Dalrymple (CF), Tom Burns (3B), Jim Clarkson (P), Billy Sunday (substitute). Billy Sunday, by the way, was the preacher who unsuccessfully tried to reform Chicago, as reflected in the Frank Sinatra song, "Chicago." Corcoran must be standing on a box, since he was only 5'3".**

Kelly may have been known primarily for his base stealing ability, but he could also really hit. For example, he led the league in batting for

---

[15] http://fromdeeprightfield.com/

the first time in 1884, hitting .354 for the season. Kelly won the batting crown once again in 1886, a year that could be considered his best. Both batting titles were with the White Stockings. Over the season, he hit .388, and also led the National League with 155 runs scored and a .483 on-base percentage.

But not all was well in Chicago. Kelly was always unhappy with his pay–partly because Spalding was a shrewd businessman–and partly because Kelly always managed to spend more than he made. Spalding finally had enough, and sold his most popular player to the National League's Boston franchise after the 1886 season for the unheard of sum of $10,000! That was like Albert Pujols-type money today.

## Career after the White Stockings

In front of sold-out crowds in Boston, Kelly continued to perform at a high level. He averaged a .308 batting average for his 16 year career (1878-1893), hit 69 home runs, and scored 1,357 runs. He tallied 950 RBIs, and recorded 1,813 hits. Kelly is also credited with designing the parameters for the hit-and-run, a key component of "small ball" offense. This style of aggressive "small ball" was carried to a new level by Ned Hanlon's Baltimore Orioles, featuring third baseman John McGraw and shortstop Hughie Jennings (both to be later enshrined in Cooperstown).

Interestingly enough, perhaps because of Kelly, baseball began adding more umpires per game. When Kelly first became a pro, there was only one umpire on the field per game. Many times, if Kelly came to the plate with runners in scoring position–and got a hit–there would usually be an attempt to throw out the base runner at home plate. Knowing that the umpire would be occupied making the call at home plate, Kelly would cut across the field, completely bypassing third base and slide into home plate just behind the already sliding base runner (that Kelly had just knocked in). Invariably, both runners would be called safe. No matter that the opposing team would scream to the umpire that Kelly hadn't touched third base–the umpire didn't see it, therefore, Kelly was safe. The fans took to chanting "Slide, Kelly, Slide!" whenever Kelly was on base, causing great angst to the opposing team. All this did was to make King Kelly into an even bigger star. The fans of his team loved him. As a result, Major League administrators added more umpires to each game in an attempt to "level" the playing field.

Another rules change, attributed to Kelly's actions, occurred in 1891, when Kelly was player-manager for the Boston franchise. During an exhibition game against Philadelphia's National League franchise, Ed Delahanty, one of the most feared clutch-hitters in baseball (and a future Hall of Famer), came to the plate with 2 outs and the bases loaded. On the first pitch, Delahanty lofted a foul pop to the area in front of the Boston (first base) dugout. Kelly had been sitting on the dugout bench. He suddenly jumped out onto the field and yelled, "Kelly now catching for Boston!"–and promptly caught the ball for the third out. This incident caused the Major League's rules committee to require that all substitutions be acknowledged by the home plate umpire before the pitch is thrown, a practice now followed in all sports – checking in with the umpire or referee first..

As King Kelly became an ever bigger star in Boston, fans bought him an expensive home as well as a horse and carriage. Crowds followed him everywhere. In 1888, Kelly published his autobiography, entitled "Play Ball: Stories of the Ball Field," ghostwritten by Boston Globe reporter John Drohan. The book sold well. In 1888, Ernest Thayer published his iconic American classic poem, "Casey at the Bat". It has always been rumored that Thayer's "Casey" was modeled after King Kelly. As one fan was reputed to have said, "Kelly's strikeouts are more exciting than other players' hits!"[16]

A song writer named J. W. Kelly (no relation), in 1889, penned a song, "Slide, Kelly, Slide!", highlighting the excitement generated by Kelly's base running. It became the biggest hit tune of the 19th century. Vaudeville productions resulted (some starring Kelly himself), increasing Kelly's fame. Believe it or not, as late as 1927, a movie called "Slide, Kelly, Slide!" became popular, too. To put Kelly in perspective, perhaps only Babe Ruth ever approached Kelly's

---

[16] http://fromdeeprightfield.com/

popularity in baseball history. No one else in baseball history stood out from their peers in the way Kelly and Ruth did.

Experts often wondered what Kelly's stats would have looked like if he had taken better care of himself. He loved having a good time as much as he loved the game–and partied and drank way too much. He was given to unpredictable moods, accompanied by (or, attributed to) frequent hangovers. He was uncompromisingly self-destructive in his personal habits…and it wore his health down.

In the Fall of 1894, Kelly was in New York performing at a theater. He left New York City on Sunday, November 4, 1894, and traveled by boat to Boston. A snowstorm hit during the journey, and Kelly took ill. Some reports have Kelly catching cold because he gave his overcoat to a freezing man on the boat. When he arrived in Boston he had chills and fever and rested at a friend's house. In this weakened state of health, Kelly caught pneumonia and passed away at age 36. At his funeral service, 7,000 fans filed past his casket. His beautiful wife, Agnes, whom he married in 1881, sadly shared, "Mike was an overgrown kid in many ways, but he was the most charitable person I ever knew." Kelly's unexpected death was front-page news in every National League city.

Baseball, however, did not forget the great King Kelly. 51 years after his death, he was elected to baseball's Hall of Fame in 1945. Kelly was the game's first matinee idol, a man who knew how to touch the fans, and how to live large.

The most popular baseball player of the 19th century, King Kelly. And he spent more seasons with the Chicago Cubs – seven - than any other team.

"Slide, Kelly, Slide."

# 6 JIMMY RYAN

I thought that Jimmy Ryan was just another decent 19th century baseball player until I started looking at his stats. Then I was very impressed!

The SABR 19th Century Committee recently polled its members to determine the top ten players of the pre-1900 era who are not in the Hall of Fame. Heading the list in a three-way tie were Jimmy Ryan, Harry Stovey, and George Van Haltren.

Ryan was an outstanding outfielder with the Chicago White Stockings in the 1880's and 1890's. Also noteworthy is that in the entire *history* of major league baseball, just two players have ever had careers of 2000 or more games, while batting right-handed and throwing left-handed: Ricky Henderson and, yes, Jimmy Ryan.[17]

Jimmy Ryan, National League leader in outfield assists.

Jimmy Ryan played for the White Stockings and their successor teams from 1885-1900, with one year off – 1890 – to play in the ill-fated Players League. He finished off his career in 1902-03 with Washington of the American League. During his career, his lifetime batting average was .308, and he had 2512 total hits at a time where

---

[17]www.BillJamesonline.com

baseball played fewer than 154 games. In 1888 – his best year - Ryan led the league in home runs, slugging percentage, doubles, hits, and was second in batting average. Not bad for a guy who topped out at 5 foot 9 inches and 162 pounds. I can certainly see why he should at least have been strongly considered for admission into Cooperstown.

Born at Clinton, Massachusetts, February 11, 1863, James E. Ryan began his baseball career at Holy Cross College, although it is not clear whether he was a student or only a member of the team. (I guess you could do that in those days, unlike today, where college athletes have to be real scholars.) In mid-1885 Ryan went professional, joining Bridgeport of the Eastern League, and had but 29 games of minor league experience when Cap Anson signed him with the Chicago White Stockings at the close of the season. Stationed at shortstop in place of Tommy Burns, Jimmy made his debut October 8, 1885, at Chicago. Although he went only one-for-four in a 5-3 loss to the Phillies, the *Chicago Tribune* noted that "Ryan, the young Bridgeport player...proved himself a strong batter, a quick fielder and very clever between the bases." The following day he went four-for-six but the Phillies again won, 12-11.

## Career with the White Stockings

In 1886, playing on a semi-regular basis, Ryan gave Chicago a glimpse of things to come by batting .306. Beginning the next year, he was an everyday player for the rest of his career.

By 1888 Jimmy was approaching his stride, hitting for both average and power with a .332 average and a league-leading 16 home runs. Generally batting in the leadoff spot, Ryan became renowned for his game opening homers – another similarity with Ricky Henderson - the first of which came April 20, 1888, in a 5-4 victory at Indianapolis. On July 28 he became the first Chicago player to hit for the cycle, collecting a single, a double, two triples and a homer as the White Stockings outslugged Detroit, 21-17. The versatile Ryan also spent 7-1/3 innings on the mound in that game at Chicago and just missed being the only pitcher to hit for the cycle because he singled and tripled before taking the mound.

In 1889 Jimmy reached a career high with 17 homers but did not lead the league because Sam Thompson of the Phillies belted 20. On September 30 Ryan hit George Haddock's first pitch for his sixth leadoff homer of the year as Chicago took care of Washington, 9-5. This remained a major league record until broken by Bobby Bonds – not his son Barry - in 1973.

By now Ryan had established himself as a bona-fide star – not only as a hitter but defensively as well. His throwing arm ranked with that of such latter-day standouts as Kiki Cuyler, Rocky Colavito, Roberto Clemente (perhaps the best ever, according to several polls), Andre Dawson, and Carl Furillo. Sportswriter Hugh Fullerton, who saw Jimmy perform countless times, recalled years later that "He was known as the most accurate and clever thrower in the history of the game." The statistics bear this out, as Jimmy made 33 assists in 1887, a league-leading 34 in `88 and a career high 36 in `89. Equally adept in left, center or right, Ryan would in time play regularly in all three spots. By the end of his career, he had played 386 games in left, 954 in center, and 606 in right. (In the 1890's, Bill Lange, the next player profiled, would generally play center field.) As a base stealer, Ryan was good (408 thefts), but not exceptional.

In addition to his offensive and defensive abilities, Jimmy was one of baseball's first successful relief pitchers at a time when relief pitchers were very uncommon. He pitched in 24 games between 1886 and 1893, winning seven games while losing only one. In 1888 his pitching record was 4-0, with three of his wins coming in relief. Although he went to bat only 55 times while pitching, he technically became baseball's greatest hitting pitcher by batting for an average of .436 and slugging at an .891 clip. His 24 hits included six doubles, two triples, and five home runs. Ryan also occasionally played infield. He played 58 games at short, 8 at second base, and 6 at third.

Personally, Ryan was a moderate to heavy drinker and a rather moody individual who didn't get along well with his fellow players, particularly Anson, the player-manager. (Seems like a lot of guys did not get along with Cap Anson). However, if failure to get along with one's teammates is a valid reason for denying entrance into the Hall of Fame, then Ty Cobb does not belong either. According to most baseball experts, everybody hated him!

In the late 1880s, the first player rebellion was in the wind. (The Federal League in 1914-1915 had a more successful player rebellion.) The first players' union, the Brotherhood of Professional Baseball Players, had been formed in 1886, and three years later they presented their demands to the National League. While the league acceded to a few minor points, they balked at the abolition of the reserve clause and the salary limitation. With very unsatisfying results for the players, they actually bolted in 1890, forming the Players' League. Since Chicago second baseman Fred Pfeffer was one of the leaders in the movement, nearly all of the White Stockings joined him, including Ryan. Most of them signed with the Chicago Players' League team, nicknamed the "Onions."[18] Although the team had a star-studded lineup, including Ryan, Pfeffer, Hugh Duffy and Charlie Comiskey, they finished only fourth as Ryan led with a .340 mark. Furthermore, the new league went bankrupt in its attempt to alter baseball's power structure.

Unlike Pfeffer – lifetime .256 hitter with 1678 hits who played most of his career with Chicago and remained a staunch unionist - Ryan emerged thoroughly disillusioned with the union and future efforts to unionize from the experience. After the Players' League folded, Ryan, Pfeffer and pitcher Ad Gumbert were returned to the Chicago Nationals, who had been renamed the Colts due to a massive influx of young players. For Ryan, 1891 was, by his standards, a sub-par season as his batting average fell to .287. But on July 1 he became the only Cub player to hit for the cycle twice, connecting in a 9-3 victory over Cleveland.

A year later to the day, Jimmy earned another distinction of sorts by becoming the first Chicago player to slug a sportswriter – as I indicated, he was somewhat moody and had a bit of a temper. It seems George Bechel of the *Chicago Evening News* had written some unkind words about Ryan's abilities, after which Jimmy taught him a

---

[18] The Onions were 75-62 in their only year, and financially, the league was a disaster.

lesson in journalistic diplomacy. By now the team was on the decline and Ryan, sporting a thick handlebar mustache, was one of the few genuine stars left in the lineup.

On August 6, 1893, Ryan suffered a severe leg injury in a train wreck at Toledo, which limited his action that year to 83 games. But that did not stop him from rebounding the following year with a .361 average, the highest of his career. Even conceding the fact that .300 hitters were a dime a dozen in 1894, Ryan's mark was still 52 points above the league average. That season he enjoyed one of his finest days as he slapped out five hits in five trips, two of them doubles, and scored six times as the Colts clobbered the Pirates, 24-6, on July 25.

Jimmy continued to excel through the 1890's. On June 29, 1897, the Colts set a major league record for runs scored when they pummeled Louisville, 36-7. Jimmy's contributions were a grand slam homer, a double and five runs scored.

The departure of Anson in 1898 left Ryan the senior member of the team, which had been relabeled "Orphans," being without their "father," Anson, who was fired. Two years earlier, Giant manager Bill Joyce had said of Ryan, "Baseball patrons in Chicago should appreciate that man, for there are no better players to be found anywhere. I have admired him for years, not only for his ability on the field but as a man." And Chicago fans did appreciate him. On April 27, 1899, at the home opener, a contingent of fans presented him a gold watch. Jimmy showed his thanks by singling in the third inning and driving in the winning run with a two-run double in the fifth as Chicago nipped the Reds, 4-3. The *Chicago Tribune* commented that "the crowd cheered his every play." For the season, the blond Irishman hit .301, for his sixth straight year over the .300 plateau. And on August 8, 1900, Jimmy stole four bases in a 5-3 loss to the Phillies for a career high. But when his average dropped to .277, the Orphans decided he was over the hill and released him.

Following a one-year tour as player-manager of the St. Paul Western League franchise, Jimmy made a comeback in 1902 with the Washington Senators of the brand new rival American League. Although Ryan was now 39 years old, his .320 batting average was the envy of most of his teammates. However, after Jimmy dropped to .249 the following year, he retired from active play. He managed Colorado Springs of the Western League in 1904, then left professional ball for keeps. (I think he would have made a good manager, but it was not to be.)

## Life after Baseball

Now that their big league days were behind them, Ryan and Pfeffer mended fences with Anson, and together they attended the 1906 World Series between the Cubs and the White Sox. But playing baseball was still in Jimmy's blood, so the following year he formed his own semi-pro team in Rogers Park, a neighborhood on Chicago's north side and not that far from the current site of Wrigley Field. He played regularly for Rogers Park as late as 1915, when he was 52!

Ryan's last public appearance came on September 16, 1923, when he and Fred Pfeffer attended the dedication of Cap Anson's monument at Oakwood Cemetery on Chicago's south side. On October 29, 1923, Ryan died of a heart attack on the front porch of his home in Rogers Park at age 60. Serving as a Cook County deputy sheriff at the time of his death, Jimmy left a widow but no children. He is buried at Calvary Cemetery in Evanston, Illinois.

If a player is best judged by comparing him to his contemporaries, then Jimmy Ryan, though relatively short in stature, stood tall. When Jimmy retired, he left behind a .308 lifetime batting average, 2,512 hits, 451 doubles, 157 triples and 118 home runs during the dead ball era when home runs were infrequent. Ryan's RBI count was limited to 1,093 by the fact that he generally hit in the leadoff position. Nevertheless, his best RBI totals were 89 in 1890, 86 in '96 and 85 in '97.

By comparison, among players who retired up to and including the year 1910, only Anson, George Van Haltren, George Davis, Big Ed Delahanty, Jesse Burkett, Jake Beckley, Lave Cross, and Willie Keeler collected more hits. Prior to the advent of the lively ball in 1920, only nine others gathered 100 or more career home runs: Harry Stovey, Dan Brouthers, Sam Thompson, Roger Connor, Ed Delahanty,

Hugh Duffy, Mike Tiernan, Honus Wagner and Gavvy Cravath. And among those, only Connor (136), Thompson (128), Stovey (120) and Cravath (119) exceeded Ryan, which places Jimmy in truly select company.[19] On the all-time Cub roster, Ryan is tenth in batting average (500-game minimum), sixth in hits, sixth in doubles, first in triples, tenth in home runs, second in runs scored, and sixth in RBI.

Finally, who leads National League outfielders in career assists? Not Willie Mays, Henry Aaron, Max Carey or Roberto Clemente. Ryan's 356 outfield assists in a Cub uniform are still the NL standard. Add to this, his Players' League and American League statistics, and his career total is 404. Tris Speaker, the all-time leader with 450, appeared in 2,700 games in the outfield compared to Ryan's 1,943.

In 1982 Jimmy was elected to the Chicago Cubs Hall of Fame by a vote of the fans. While it is gratifying that he has at least been honored locally, he is still not in the Hall of Fame in Cooperstown. Perhaps some day that will be rectified, although not likely.

---

[19] Connor and Thompson are in fact in the Hall of Fame.

# 7 BILL LANGE

I am really surprised that there has never been a movie made about the life of one William Alexander Lange.

Bill Lange is probably the least well-known player on this list, but arguably one of the best. In a career which spanned only seven seasons – 1893-1899 – all with the Cubs or Orphans as they were then known - before retiring at age 28 to go into his father-in-law's insurance business, Bill Lange had a lifetime batting average of .330, second only in Cub history to Riggs Stephenson's .334.[20]

In a major-league playing career that lasted only seven seasons, Bill Lange made an indelible impression on those who saw him in action. A star outfielder on the also-ran Chicago Colts of the 1890s –

---

[20] Batting averages were somewhat inflated during the 1890's but that is still a formidable figure.

management had taken the team apart by this time - Lange could do it all: run, throw, field, hit for average, and hit for power by the standards of his time. In the estimation of *The Sporting News'* publisher, A.H. Spink, Lange was "Tyrus Cobb enlarged, fully as great in speed, batting skill and baserunning." While many of his contemporaries placed Lange on their all-time all-star teams, sharing the outfield with the likes of Cobb, Tris Speaker, Ed Delahanty, or Joe Jackson, present-day commentators have been similarly impressed. Baseball historian Bill James has described Lange as "probably the greatest all-around athlete to play major-league baseball in the 19th century," while Lyle Spatz, Chairman of SBAR's baseball records committee, dubbed him "the Willie Mays of his day."

As if abundant playing talent were not enough, Lange was also endowed with imposing size (nearly 6-feet-2 and eventually playing at about 215 pounds), matinee-idol good looks, and an amiable, outgoing personality. Admired by fellow players, routinely hailed in the sporting press – negative newspaper comment about Lange was rare until late in his playing career – and adored by the fans, Bill Lange stood at the pinnacle of baseball success. Then at the close of the 1899 season, Lange abandoned it all, quitting the game in order to marry a girl whose well-heeled father would not tolerate a baseball player for a son-in-law. Sadly, the marriage did not last – oh well -, but Lange's departure from the diamond did. He never returned to uniform, having played his final game at the age of 28. (By comparison, Alfonso Soriano did not even sign his eight-year contract with the Cubs until age 30.)

## Early Life

William Alexander Lange was born in San Francisco on June 16, 1871, the seventh of eight children born to career soldier Charles Lange and his wife, Mary. Bill's parents were German Catholic immigrants who had moved to the American West in the 1850s, where Charles enlisted in the US Army. His various postings led to Lange children being born in California (Charles Jr., 1857), Utah (John, 1859), and Washington Territory (Mary, 1860), before Charles Sr. was posted, more or less permanently, to the Presidio, the historic military installation situated at the northern tip of San Francisco.

There, Bill and sisters Margaret (born 1863), Frances (1865), Augusta (1869), and Agnes (1875) were born. As was the case with many of his generation, Bill Lange's education ended with the eighth grade and his vocation, if any, is unknown. From his mid-teens, however, Lange attracted attention on San Francisco-area sandlots, playing for various amateur teams, including a state championship team from Santa Rosa, California.

In 1890, 19-year-old Bill Lange joined the Port Townsend (Washington) Colts, a semipro team managed by his older brother Charlie, a local saloonkeeper. After three seasons of minor league baseball in Washington State and California, in 1893 Bill Lange came to the majors, signing with the Chicago Colts/Orphans, a powerhouse during the 1880s but now a club in serious decline. Ever since the team's founding as a charter member of the National League, its teams had been dominated by star first baseman Cap Anson, the Chicago field skipper since 1879 and a two-time league batting champion. In time Lange would join the ranks of Anson tormentors. But for the time being he focused on proving his worth.

## Career with the White Stockings/Colts/Orphans

On April 27, 1893, Lange made his major-league debut. The team finished in ninth place (out of 12 teams) 56-71, as the Chicago pitching corps, particularly former ace Bill Hutchinson, proved unable to cope with the newly adopted 60-foot 6-inch hurling distance and the elimination of the pitcher's box. Although Lange batted no more than a modest .281 – just .002 over the league batting norm, pitchers included – he proved a valuable asset for manager Anson. In 117 games he hit 8 home runs, scored 92 runs, and knocked in 88 more, while his 47 stolen bases placed him in the National League's top ten. Of probably more importance was Lange's defensive versatility. He alternated between second base (57 games) and the outfield (40 games), while filling in occasionally at third, shortstop, and at catcher. All in all, Lange had made a favorable first impression, and better days were yet to come.

Permanently shifted to center field, where his speed and throwing arm could be put to better use, Lange established himself as a major league star the following season. Given the offensive explosion of 1894 – the National League batted .310 as a whole that year – Lange's .325 batting average was unremarkable. Indeed, on the Colts alone, Anson (.388), Jimmy Ryan (.361), Bill Dahlen (.357), and Walt Wilmot (.330) all posted higher averages. But an athlete's physique and a friendly swagger on the field were drawing attention to Big Bill Lange. And in one category, he was clearly coming to the fore: baserunning. A combination of speed, intimidating size, and reckless base path abandon would make Lange "the toughest, roughest base runner who ever strode the bases" (Clark Griffith), "as good as Ty Cobb" (Frank Chance), and "the greatest [base runner] I ever saw," (Connie Mack). For the 1894 Colts, Lange stole 66 bases, tops on the league-leading (327 steals) Colts and fifth place in individual National League player rankings. But the Colts overall were little improved, their season-ending 57-75 log ensuring another second-division placement. (As Harry Caray would say, "What about the pitching?").

The 1895 season saw Lange at the peak of his performance on offense. Playing in 123 games, he established personal bests in runs scored (120), doubles (27), triples (16), homers (10), total bases (275), batting average (.389), on-base percentage (.456), slugging average (.575), and OPS (1.032). He also stole 67 bases while playing standout defense in center. With solid contributions from the now 43-year-old Anson (.335), rookie third baseman Bill Everitt (.358), and right-hander Clark Griffith (26-14), the Colts returned to respectability, posting a winning (72-58) record for the first time in four years. But from there, things would turn sour in Chicago, with Lange contributing to a toxic clubhouse atmosphere that eventually prompted Anson's termination as team leader.

A natural showman who reveled in the limelight – the strut that he affected is sometimes cited as a basis for his being given the nickname of "Little Eva" (the scandalous "hoochie-coochie" girl of the Nile at the 1893 Colombian Exposition in Chicago) – Bill Lange was the darling of the Chicago fandom, a landslide winner in a 1895 *Chicago Tribune* poll of the fans' favorite player. Handsome, gregarious, and a fun-loving ladies' man, Bill was also a hit in Chicago saloons and boudoirs. With shortstop Bill Dahlen and other like-minded teammates often in tow, Lange was the backbone of the

Colts' "Dawn Patrol," skipping curfews, missing trains, and generally ignoring authority. Inevitably this created friction on the club, particularly with the cheerless sourpuss Cap Anson, a favorite target of the practical jokes relished by his more rowdy players. (Maybe the team would have had a better record if they had played in Rockford or Peoria instead of Chicago.)

Notwithstanding his frequent late nights, Big Bill turned in another first-rate season statistically in 1896. He batted .326, with 114 runs scored and 92 RBIs. He tied his personal best of 16 triples and stole 84 bases, still the Chicago single-season record. Perhaps even more impressive was Lange's play in center field. He led National League outfielders with 355 total chances.

The Colts maintained respectability in 1896, their 71-57 record good for another first-division finish. But the attitude of certain Colts had not gone unnoticed. Even before the 1897 season began, John McGraw of the pennant-winning Baltimore Orioles publicly lambasted Lange, Dahlen, and Jimmy Ryan for their disrespectful treatment of field leader Anson (whom McGraw also criticized for tolerating it). Perhaps as a result, the team got off to a sluggish start, with many Colts playing indifferently when not in outright defiance of Anson's instructions. By late June, Chicago had plummeted to 11th place, and when a tough loss to Pittsburgh was followed by joking and tomfoolery at the train station, Anson exploded. He loudly denounced his players as "a bunch of loafers and drunkards" bent on throwing him down. Publication of the remarks, which Anson virtually demanded, sealed his fate. The Colts limped home 57-73 (ninth place), and the following February Anson's annual contract was not renewed, bringing the tenure of the longtime Chicago leader to a rather inglorious end.

From a statistical standpoint, the team turmoil had had little effect on Lange. He had scored 119 runs in 118 games and batted .340, tops on the club. His 73 stolen bases were the most in the league, the only time that Lange would ever lead the National League in an offensive department. But the Windy City's love affair with Big Bill was about to be put to the test. After surviving the offseason trade rumors that annually swirled about him, Lange was passed over as field captain.

New Chicago manager Tom Burns instead opted for a curious alternative: Bill Dahlen, a genuine talent but a man of such sullen and insubordinate disposition that he was known as Bad Bill. Predictably, Dahlen proved an unsuitable choice, terrorizing umpires on the field while constantly feuding with club management and otherwise making himself utterly disagreeable. Lange, meanwhile, had to contend with physical and attitude problems. Notwithstanding his youth and impressive physique, Lange had never been a particularly durable player, regularly missing a dozen or so games over the course of a season due to minor injuries.

In 1898 the condition became more chronic, with leg and foot miseries keeping Lange out of the Chicago lineup for extended stretches. His demeanor compounded the problem; he seemed indifferent to his responsibilities to the club and took additional time off to attend to personal business (basically to sneak off to the racetrack). Fed up, management suspended Lange without pay until he got himself back into playing condition, while Chicago's once fawning press turned on him. Chastened, Lange refocused his attentions on baseball and, by the end of the season had compiled respectable numbers. In a year where offensive statistics were down league-wide, Lange batted .319. But otherwise, his production was considerably diminished from the previous year. Among other things, Lange managed only 32 extra-base hits and swiped a career-low 22 bases.

In the offseason, Chicago club president James Hart publicly endorsed growing sentiment for change in the team roster, singling out Dahlen and Lange by name as candidates to be traded. "As for Lange, I admire his playing and like him personally. He is a good, bright fellow, and a nice man to meet socially. Lange was criticized last year where he did not deserve it. I will say that for him, but he at times showed a lack of regard for the welfare of the club that could not be forgiven, especially in its effect upon the public."

In January 1899 Dahlen was shipped to Brooklyn in exchange for shortstop Gene DeMontreville. Lange, however, remained Chicago property, working himself into top condition and playing a few games for the Watsonville club of an early Pacific Coast League. As the

1899 season approached, Lange's status with the Orphans (as the Chicago club had been branded following Anson's severance) remained unsettled. But the baseball future of Bill Lange was no longer in the hands of Chicago's team management. Rather, it would be shaped by a wealthy and socially ambitious San Francisco insurance/property management mogul named William Giselman. Over the winter Lange had been smitten by Giselman's only daughter, a 21-year-old beauty named Grace Anna, and a courtship had ensued. Like many a serious business-minded immigrant, the German-born William Giselman had little use for professional baseball players, and certainly no intention of having one in the family. Accordingly, any engagement to Grace would be conditioned upon Lange's abandonment of the game following the 1899 season and his taking up the insurance/real estate business that Giselman would set Bill up in. Lange agreed. Thereafter, in early March 1899, the Chicago sports world was stunned by the announcement that playboy Bill Lange was engaged to be married and that the coming campaign would be his last in a baseball uniform.

As his final season approached, Lange became embroiled in a decision over who should be field captain of the team.[21] With the seconding of club president Hart, manager Burns had named Jimmy Ryan, senior in playing service to the team and friendly with the front office. The players promptly rebelled, most demanding that the honor go to Lange and threatening to refuse to take the field behind Ryan for the coming opener against Louisville. Burns immediately caved in. The Ryan appointment was rescinded and the Orphans played the game (and the ensuing season) without a formally designated captain.

As it turned out, Big Bill would have made a poor field leader. Although he had worked hard to put himself in peak condition, Lange's body again broke down. Leg injuries and a bad back necessitated prolonged time out of the lineup. Exasperated, club management suspended Lange until he could take the field again. In time, Lange recovered sufficiently to play out the season. On the

---

[21] Generally speaking, on-the-field captains were common at that time but have been eliminated in modern baseball.

night after the last game, a small group of friends and teammates gathered for a farewell dinner at a Chicago restaurant. Emceeing the festivities was Cap Anson who, like most everyone else, had not been able to stay angry with Bill Lange for very long. Then, "the most popular man who ever wore a Chicago uniform" was gone, departed from the diamond scene at the youthful age of 28. But Lange's final season had borne more evidence of athletic decline. Able to appear in only 107 games, Lange hit .325, but with reduced power numbers, including only one home run and a mere 58 RBIs. The condition of his legs, moreover, had required a change of position for this once peerless outfielder to first base for 14 games.

## Life after Baseball

Bill Lange would live another 50 years. But he would never play another major-league baseball game. At first the hope persisted that he could be induced to return, a wish nurtured by less-than-definitive Lange remarks about his intentions. The door to a baseball comeback seemed to shut, however, on April 15, 1900 when William Alexander Lange and Grace Anna Giselman were married at St. Dominic's Roman Catholic Church in San Francisco.

For the next several years, reports that Lange was negotiating a baseball return were published regularly, but nothing ever came of it. The insurance/real estate business afforded him a comfortable living and Lange traveled frequently, often in connection with the game that he could never shake from his system. In October 1910 he returned to Chicago for the first time in 11 years for the Cubs-Athletics World Series and was warmly received. The following year, Lange accepted a California scouting position for the Cincinnati Reds. He also served as West Coast representative for the National Commission, organized baseball's governing body, and was mentioned for the presidency of the Pacific Coast League, a top-notch minor league.[22] In 1913 Lange was finally coaxed back into uniform, serving as spring-training outfield instructor for the Chicago White Sox, managed by his old friend and teammate Jimmy Callahan.

---

[22] The Pacific Coast League has been in business since 1903 and currently has 16 teams as members, including the Iowa Cubs.

Sadly, things did not go as well in Bill's personal life. His marriage to Grace was childless, and in time the couple grew apart. They divorced in April 1915, by which time Bill had taken up residence at San Francisco's posh Olympic Club. At the conclusion of World War I, Lange headed to Europe as YMCA athletic director, bringing stores of baseball equipment to occupying forces. While there, he served as a talent scout for Ban Johnson[23] and John McGraw before coming to the conclusion that Europe, France in particular, would never be fertile soil for baseball – why am I not surprised? Upon his return in August 1919, Lange remarried. That marriage was short-lived but a third try at matrimony proved the charm for Bill Lange. On September 9, 1925, he married Sara Griffith, and some three years later Lange became a father for the first and only time at age 56, a son named William Alexander Lange, Jr.

In later life Bill lived quietly in the San Francisco suburb of Burlingame until Sara's death in January 1948. He then returned to his rooms at the Olympic Club. There, he suffered a fatal heart attack on July 13, 1950. Bill Lange was 79.

News of Lange's passing brought forth tributes from remaining contemporaries, including venerable Washington Senators club owner Clark Griffith, a teammate in the 1890s. Said Griffith: "I have seen all the other great outfielders – Speaker, Cobb, DiMaggio – in action, and I consider Bill Lange the equal of, if not better than, all outfielders of all time. There wasn't anything he couldn't do." Lange registered impressive offensive numbers, as well: a .330 career lifetime batting average, with extra-base power. He also stole an extraordinary 400 bases in only 813 games played. But his major-league tenure was brief, far short of the ten-year minimum required for Hall of Fame consideration, and injury-plagued toward the end.

Notwithstanding these shortcomings, Bill Lange was a gifted and colorful ballplayer, one who lingered in public consciousness long after his all-too-brief playing days were over.

---

[23] Ban Johnson was founder and first president of the American League.

**1896 Chicago Colts/Orphans – Bill Lange is in the middle row, fourth from the left**

# 8 MORDECAI (THREE FINGER) BROWN

Here is something that will probably be a huge surprise to most Cub fans, especially younger ones. The greatest pitcher in Chicago Cubs history is not Ferguson Jenkins, Greg Maddux (most of his great years were in fact with the Atlanta Braves), Bruce Sutter, or any of the more modern Chicago Cubs, but a fellow who pitched in the early 1900's named Mordecai Peter Centennial Brown. Brown led the Cubs to four National League pennants and two – count them, two! - World Series championships in 1907 and 1908.

Sporting a lifetime record of 239-130 and an ERA of 2.08, most of which was with the Cubs, Brown is regarded as one of the premier pitchers of the first few decades of the 1900's. In addition, he led the league in saves from 1908-1911, which further demonstrates his overall value to the team. His battles with one of the greatest pitchers of all time, Christy Mathewson of the Giants, are legendary. At one point in his career, Brown beat Mathewson nine straight times, showing just how good the man with the missing finger was.

Mordecai Peter Centennial Brown, best known today for his unusual name and his more or less descriptive nickname of "Three Finger," was the ace right-hander of the great Chicago Cub teams of the first decade or so of the twentieth century. With Brown leading an extraordinary pitching staff, the Cubs from 1906 through 1910 put together the greatest five-year record of any team in baseball history – note that folks! We are talking about the Chicago Cubs here! His battles with the Giants' Mathewson epitomized the bitter rivalry between the two best teams in the National League at that time.

Brown was born October 19, 1876, in the farming community of Nyesville, Indiana. His parents, Jane (also known as Louisa) and Peter Brown, moved the family from Kentucky to Indiana prior to Mordecai's birth. Because the year of his birth was our country's centennial, Mordecai was given an extra middle name. Although it is generally assumed that the quite religious Browns chose their son's names from the Bible, Peter was his father's name, and there was an uncle named Mordecai. The family claimed to be of Welsh and English descent, but genealogical records indicate there may have been some Cherokee Indian heritage as well. Brown was five feet ten inches tall and weighed 175 pounds in his playing days, good sized but certainly not large, even in the early 1900's.

Then there's that nickname – Three Finger Brown. This is somewhat of an error, because he actually had four and a half fingers on his pitching hand. Because of childhood curiosity, Mordecai lost most of his right index finger in a piece of farming equipment. Not long after, he fell while chasing a rabbit and broke his other fingers. The result was a bent middle finger, a paralyzed little finger, and a stump where the index finger used to be. Generally not a pleasant situation but actually an extra advantage in throwing a baseball – Based on what I have seen of Cub pitchers over the past 50+ years, maybe more of them should have lost a finger. Mordecai's other nickname also described him. He was called Miner Brown because he worked in the coal mines when he was a teenager.

In those days the working people found relief from the daily grind by playing baseball. The mining towns near Mordecai's home had their own teams, and Mordecai played for Clinton, Shelburn, and Coxville. While playing third base for Coxville, Mordecai was called on to fill in for Coxville's regular pitcher against the neighboring town of Brazil. The year was 1898, and the pitcher's absence turned into a blessing for Mordecai (and eventually the Cubs!)

Brown's deformed hand enabled him to throw a bewildering pitch with lots of movement. Although the jumping ball was a problem when Brown was an infielder, it was an advantage when he pitched. Despite having what had seemed like a terrible handicap, Brown's pitching performance that day was daunting. The Brazil manager was impressed, and the team offered Brown more money to play for them, but he didn't jump until he'd completed the season.

In 1901 Mordecai, with the help of six hundred fans who threatened to boycott the games if he didn't make the team, secured a spot on the Terre Haute Tots in the newly formed Three-I league – Illinois, Indiana, and Iowa, if I recall correctly. Mordecai led the semiprofessional team to the first-ever Three-I championship, posting a 25-8 record. Brown was picked up by Omaha in the Western League the following year, and reporters started calling him Three Finger. He became the staff workhorse, posting a 27-15 record and finishing every game he started – not unusual in those days, by the way.

After that season in Omaha, Mordecai joined the St. Louis Cardinals in 1903. His major league debut for St. Louis, against the Cubs, of course, was similar to the outing in Coxville. In both games Brown pitched five innings, and his dominance over hitters was obvious to all observers. While his rookie record was not impressive, 9-13, it should be remembered that St. Louis was the last-place team that year in the National League, 46 1/2 games back. Brown's earned run average was the lowest on the team at 2.60, and his nine wins tied veteran Chappie McFarland for most on the team.

Mordecai and Christy Mathewson began their famous face-offs during Mordecai's rookie year. The first time they met, on July 9, they dueled through eight innings, not allowing a run. In the ninth inning the Giants got to Mordecai for three runs and beat the Cardinals 4-2.

After the 1903 season, Brown and pitcher Jack O'Neill were traded to the Chicago Cubs, the team Mordecai beat in his rookie appearance and the team for which he would set records that have not been broken to date. The Cardinals received veteran pitcher Jack Taylor, who was suspected of throwing games, and rookie catcher Larry McLean. The Cardinals, being the last-place team, were probably desperate for an experienced pitcher, and Mordecai had not yet proven himself. It was the Cubs, however, who benefited the most by the trade because Mordecai had his greatest years while pitching for Chicago. By the way, this was probably one of the worst trades in Cardinal history and might soften the blow of the Brock for Broglio trade 60 years later – the worst trade in the history of the Chicago Cubs.

That off season, Brown married 22-year-old Sarah Burgham on December 17, 1903, in Rosedale, Indiana, shortly before he joined the Cubs. The marriage lasted forty-five years, until Mordecai's death. Sarah died ten years later on Oct. 5, 1958. They had no children.

After joining the Cubs in 1904, Mordecai improved his record to 15-10 and lowered his ERA to 1.86. Brown still holds the Cubs record for most shutouts (since 1900) with 48 and lowest career ERA of 1.80. In addition, Brown is the Cubs' post-1900 record holder for most wins in a season, 29 in 1908, and the lowest earned run average (ERA) in a season, 1.04 in 1906. When Mordecai joined the club he was already twenty-seven years old, the same age as his manager, Frank Chance, and older than most of his fellow players.

Mordecai's greatest years were during his tenure with the Cubs, 1904 to 1912, when he won 186 games and had six straight seasons, from 1905 to 1910, posting 20 or more wins – that's why he is in this book, after all. During that time he led the Cubs to two World Series championships.

His best year was probably 1906 when he was 26-6 and a winning percentage of .813. He pitched nine shutouts that year, and his 1.04

ERA is baseball's third best in a single season. The Cubs won a remarkable 116 games in 1906 but lost the World Series to their cross-town rival White Sox, known as the Hitless Wonders because the team's batting average was a weak .230. Mordecai won one of the World Series games, but one he lost, Game 6, 8-3, lifted his series ERA to 3.66.

The following year was also a good one for Three Finger. In 1907 he posted a 20-6 record and an ERA of 1.39. That year the Cubs did win the World Series, beating the Detroit Tigers in five games, plus one tie. In that series Mordecai pitched in only Game 5, winning 2-0.

Brown continued his winning ways. In 1908 Mordecai posted an ERA of 1.47, second only to Christy Mathewson's 1.43. But when anyone asked him when his greatest game occurred, he would always say October 8, 1908 at New York's Polo Grounds. In John P. Carmichael's *My Greatest Day in Baseball*, Mordecai said, "I was about as good that day as I ever was in my life." That was the day the Giants and Cubs met for a playoff game to determine the National League championship.

The game was made necessary because of the famous "Bonehead Merkle Play." In the ninth inning during the September 23, 1908, game between the Giants and the Cubs, young Fred Merkle failed to touch second base on a play that should have scored the winning run for the Giants. Johnny Evers, remembering a similar play earlier when the call had not gone his way, yelled for the ball that Al Bridwell had hit. Whether he got that ball or another one is uncertain, but he stood jumping up and down on second base until he captured the umpire's attention. Merkle was called out because the runner on first – Merkel – never touched second base, resulting in a force play, not a run. Because the field was overrun by fans who thought the game was over, the National League decided the game would be declared a tie, only to be replayed at the end of the season if it became necessary. It did become necessary, unfortunately for Fred Merkle.[24] At the end of the season the Chicago Cubs and the New

[24] Merkle actually had a good career in baseball, playing over 14 seasons and compiling 1500+ hits. He even played for the Cubs.

York Giants were deadlocked at the top of the National League standings.

In Mordecai's *How to Pitch Curves*, an instructional manual written for young boys and published by Chicagoan W.D. Boyce, Brown referred to that playoff game as a time when having nerve served him well in baseball. He had plenty of "pluck," as he put it, to pitch in front of a hostile crowd after receiving death threats. Gambling was commonplace in those days, and many had bet an awfully lot on that game.

Jack Pfeister started the game for Chicago, and Christy Mathewson started for New York, a repeat of the Merkle game match-up. Mordecai had started or relieved in 11 of the Cubs' last 14 games so Manager Frank Chance decided not to start his ace. The crowd was enormous; some accounts put the total at 250,000 spectators, taking into account the throng outside the gates. While that number is highly unlikely, people did fill every available space inside and outside the Polo Grounds, lining fence tops, sitting on the elevated train platform, and perching on housetops.

The Giants rocked Pfeister in the first inning, scoring their first run. Not willing to take any chances, Frank Chance called on Mordecai. Pushing through the overflow crowd, Brown made his way in from the outfield bullpen and went on to win his 29th regular season game, securing the Chicago Cubs a third straight pennant and sending them on to play the Detroit Tigers and Ty Cobb in the World Series.

The following World Series must have seemed anticlimactic. Despite the opener in which Chicago scored five in the ninth to win 10-6--a win Mordecai received after relieving in the 8th inning--there were no amazing feats to compare with the October 8 playoff game. Mordecai also won Game four, 3-0. Detroit won only Game 3 even with Ty Cobb, American League batting champion, batting .368 in the series. The final game still holds the record for the lowest fan attendance in a World Series game. Only 6,210 Detroit fans showed up to see the Cubs defeat the Tigers. (They must have known the series was over against those mighty Chicago Cubs!)

The rivalry continued between Brown and Christy Mathewson throughout their careers. Brown lost to Mathewson on June 13, 1905, a no-hitter for Matty, but after that he beat the Giants' star nine consecutive times. The ninth game was the October 8th replay of the Merkle game.

The Cubs in those days were a rowdy bunch. Fights in the clubhouse were common, sometimes landing players in the hospital. But Brown was well respected. A search in Brown's file at the National Baseball Hall of Fame produced a quote from teammate Johnny Evers. Evers described Brown as having "plenty of nerve, ability, and willingness to work under any conditions. He was charitable and friendly to his foes."

Following three more outstanding seasons between 1909 and 1911, in which he won 73 games and led the Cubs to the 1910 World Series, by 1912 Brown's career was clearly in decline. By that time he was thirty-five and only appeared in fifteen games, posting a 5-6 record. After the 1912 season, ailing from a knee injury, Mordecai was traded to the Cincinnati Reds, where he went 11-12. In 1914 Mordecai joined with other big leaguers and jumped to the short-lived Federal League. There he was player/manager for the St. Louis team before going to Brooklyn. Between the two teams he was 14-11 with a swelling ERA of 3.52. When he joined the Chicago Federals in 1915, he improved to 17-8 with an ERA of 2.09, and his team won a championship. When the Federal League folded, Brown returned to the Cubs. But at age thirty-nine he made only twelve appearances, winning two games and losing three. His ERA was his highest ever at 3.91. Mordecai's final game in the majors was September 4, 1916, the final face-off against rival Christy Mathewson, now pitcher and manager for the Cincinnati Reds.

With his big league years behind him, Mordecai accepted an invitation from his old Cub teammate, Joe Tinker, now manager of the Columbus Senators of the AAA Minor League American Association, to pitch in Ohio's capital. Brown was forty years old by then and posted a 10-12 record. Mordecai filled in as manager whenever Tinker was out scouting players. An article in the July 11, 1918, *Columbus Citizen*, notes that while playing in Louisville,

Mordecai received more applause than the home team did. His popularity may in part explain the large fan attendance Columbus enjoyed while he played there. In 1917 the Senators drew just under 105,000--in a city with a population not much larger than that. In 1918 he appeared in only thirteen games, but that was a year shortened by war and the flu outbreak.

Later in life Mordecai owned and operated a gas station in Terre Haute, Indiana. He remained popular, occasionally showing up in newspaper reports about old-timer games or columns about players' lives after baseball.

In his fourteen years in the majors, Brown won 239 games and lost only 130. He led the league in wins once, in 1909, and led the league with most shutouts in 1906 and 1910. He had a lifetime ERA of 2.06 and from 1905 to 1910 he posted 20 or more wins--numbers sparking the attention of the Hall of Fame Committee on Baseball Veterans. He was elected in 1949. But Brown didn't live to see it because he died on February 14, 1948 in Terre Haute, Indiana at the age of seventy-one.

Forty-six years after Mordecai Brown died, his relatives, led by great-nephews Joe and Fred Massey, erected a three-foot-high granite stone to mark the birthplace of Nyesville, Indiana's most famous son. On July 9, 1994, on land donated by farmer David Grindley, family and friends of the legendary three-fingered pitcher gathered to remember him.

I happened to call the chamber of commerce/tourism bureau for the county in which Brown's gravestone is located. In addition to expounding about the many covered bridges in their county – Parke County, Indiana – they mentioned the Mordecai Brown gravestone. Yes, it is there, and we all know about it, they basically said, but if you don't look quickly, you might miss it.

In case you never get to travel to Parke County, Indiana, here is a picture of the Mordecai Brown gravesite.

All in all, Brown was an outstanding clutch pitcher, and most likely the greatest pitcher the Chicago Cubs have ever had.

**The Great Mordecai "Three Finger" Brown**

# 9 ED REULBACH

In the early 1900's, the Chicago Cubs won four pennants in five years – 1906 through 1908 and 1910 – and two world championships – 1907 and 1908. That came about primarily because they had an outstanding pitching staff.

If we assume – correctly - that Mordecai Brown was the ace of the Cub staff, then right hander Ed Reulbach must be considered as 1A. His record during those five seasons was 19-4, 17-4, 24-7, 19-10, and 12-8, for a five-year total of 91-33! Who wouldn't like to have a number two starter like Big Ed Reulbach?

The Cubs had some great pitching on those 1906-1910 teams – Orval Overall, Carl Lundgren, Jack Pfiester, and Jack Taylor come to mind. But Three Finger Brown and Big Ed Reulbach - (six foot one and close to 200 pounds) – were clearly the best. One expert called Reulbach "one of the greatest pitchers that the National League ever produced, and one of the finest, clean-cut gentlemen who ever wore a big league uniform."[25] (Good thing he did not play with King Kelly and those White Stocking teams of the 1880's!)

Reulbach employed the technique of "shadowing"—hiding the ball in his windup—as well as a high leg kick like that of Juan Marichal of a more recent era (I remember Marichal's delivery clearly, with that big leg kick). Big Ed also had what was generally regarded as the finest curve ball in either league, which allowed him to become one of baseball's most difficult pitchers to hit. He hurled two one-hitters, six two-hitters, and 13 three-hitters, and in 1906 he yielded 5.33 hits per nine innings, still the third-lowest ratio of all time. Reulbach also gave up fewer hits than innings pitched in each of his 13 seasons, a feat that was never accomplished by any pitcher in the Hall of Fame (Christy Mathewson and Cy Young also did it 13 times, but they pitched 17 and 22 seasons, respectively), and on September 26, 1908, he became the only pitcher ever to throw a doubleheader shutout.

Despite statistics that compare with those of Sandy Koufax, who also pitched in a pitching-oriented era, Reulbach never received a single vote for the Hall of Fame. Perhaps one of the factors that prevented him from receiving more consideration was his occasional lack of control. In 1920 Reulbach revealed a secret that he had been keeping for two decades: he had a weak left eye, which not only interfered with his ability to field balls hit to his left, but also sometimes made him wild. "There were times when the weak eye was worse than usual, especially on hot, gray days, or when the dust was blowing from the field," Ed recalled. "Lots of times the sweat and heat would affect the good eye and I'd have to figure out where the plate was." Reulbach said that his teammates never suspected the problem; he didn't even inform his own catchers so they could give him a special target. His walks to innings ratio is .338, or about three per nine innings – which is certainly not bad.

Edward Marvin Reulbach was born in Detroit, Michigan on December 1, 1882. Eighteen-year-old Ed was already a veteran of

---

[25] J.C. Kofoed of *Baseball Magazine*

one minor-league season with Sedalia of the Missouri Valley League, when he enrolled at the University of Notre Dame in the fall of 1901. Reulbach played interhall football and basketball and was one of the team's top hitters in a pre-season exhibition series against the reigning American League champion Chicago White Sox (The White Sox finished first in 1901 but there was as yet no World Series until 1903), but the Notre Dame faculty declared him ineligible for the 1902 college season—not because he was a professional but because he was merely a freshman. Returning to pitch for Sedalia for each of the next two summers, Ed became Notre Dame's star outfielder and pitcher, breaking the college's single-season record for strikeouts in 1904 and never yielding more than six hits in a game that season. In June his teammates elected him Captain for 1905, a popular selection according to *The Scholastic*, the Notre Dame student magazine.

While pitching for the Montpelier-Barre Hyphens of Vermont's outlaw Northern League, he met his future wife, Mary Ellen "Nellie" Whelan of Montpelier. To be closer to Nellie, Ed decided to forego his senior year at Notre Dame and enroll in medical school at the University of Vermont – apparently you could do that in 1905. In the spring he became the star of the UVM baseball team, batting cleanup and playing left field when he wasn't pitching. Newspapers called Reulbach the "greatest of all college pitchers," and on May 12, after winning his fourth start, 1-0, against Syracuse, he received an offer from the Chicago Cubs that "would take the breath away from an average person," according to the *Burlington Free Press*. (Where were these scouts when I started following the Cubs?) That night, accompanied by a large group of students, Ed caught the train to New York.

Four days later he made his major-league debut for the North Siders at the Polo Grounds against the reigning NL-champion New York Giants, tossing a complete game and giving up only five hits in a 4-0 loss. Nine days after that he earned his first victory, entering in the second inning and yielding five hits and no runs the rest of the way as the Cubs rallied to beat the Phillies, 9-4. Perhaps Ed's most impressive performance that season came against the Phillies on August 24, when he went the distance to defeat Tully Sparks, 2-1, in a 20-inning game. For the 1905 season the 22-year-old rookie posted an 18-14 record, a 1.42 ERA, and only 208 hits allowed in 290.2 innings (6.42 per nine innings).

Reulbach remained one of the NL's most dominant pitchers through 1909 and was 12-8 when the Cubs won the pennant in 1910. In 1906 he pitched 12 low-hit games (five hits or fewer), not including the one-hitter he threw against the White Sox in Game Two of that year's World Series, and started a 17-game personal winning streak that didn't end until June 29, 1907, when Deacon Phillippe of the Pittsburgh Pirates defeated him, 2-1. It was the post-1900 record for consecutive victories until Rube Marquard broke it in 1911-12, and it remains the fourth-longest streak in history.

Reulbach also set an NL record with 44 consecutive scoreless innings late in the 1908 season and led the league in winning percentage each season from 1906 to 1908, a feat matched only by Lefty Grove. On May 30, 1909, Reulbach went on a 14-game winning streak, becoming the only 20th-century NL pitcher with two winning streaks as long as 14 games. He defeated every NL team, including five wins over the Brooklyn Superbas (later the Dodgers), before he lost again on August 14. A November 1913 article in *Baseball Magazine* judged Reulbach's 1909 streak the most impressive in history; in 14 games he surrendered only 14 runs, giving up three on one occasion, while pitching five shutouts and five one-run games. One of the wins came on June 30, 1909, in the first game ever played at Pittsburgh's Forbes Field.

Reulbach's magnificent five-year run finally ended in 1910, when he tailed off to 12-8 with a 3.12 ERA in only 173.1 innings; he and Nellie had one child, a son, and Ed missed part of the season to be at his son's bedside during an attack of diphtheria. Reulbach improved to 16-9 with a 2.96 ERA in 1911, but the following year his record dipped to 10-6 while his ERA ballooned to 3.78. In July 1913, with his record a mere 1-3 to go along with a 4.42 ERA, the Cubs practically gave him to Brooklyn for cash and a mediocre pitcher named Eddie Stack. In his first six days with his new team, Reulbach proved that he still could pitch by giving up only two hits in 16 innings. Over the second half he posted a 7-6 record and 2.05 ERA, but the most telling sign that he had returned to form was his ratio of hits per nine innings: a typically Reulbachian 6.30 (77 hits in 110 innings). Reulbach's stellar second half earned him the starting assignment on Opening Day 1914, when he defeated that year's eventual World Series Champions, the Boston Braves. Despite his 11-18 record, the veteran right-hander was Brooklyn's second-best pitcher in 1914, compiling a 2.64 ERA in 256 innings.

Off the field, Reulbach was the secretary and one of the founding members of the short-lived Baseball Players' Fraternity – an early forerunner of the Major League Players Association. One of his ideas was for major leaguers to sign a pledge of total abstinence from alcohol – I can imagine that was not very popular with a lot of players! On the other hand, his efforts to raise player salaries were more popular with his colleagues than his views on alcohol consumption, but they may have cost him his job with Brooklyn. One day during the 1914 season, owner Charlie Ebbets – whom the field was named after - offered team captain Jake Daubert a $500 raise for the coming year. An excited Daubert told Reulbach while the team was en route to Chicago, but Ed advised Jake not to sign right away, figuring that the Federal League would offer even more when the train arrived in Chicago. Daubert refused to sign until Ebbets increased his offer to $9,000 per year for five years, a whopping raise of $5,000 per year. Reulbach himself was offered a big contract from the Feds, possibly as an incentive to induce other teammates to sign, but Ed declined. He ended up signing with the Feds anyway because Ebbets released him after learning that he was a ringleader in the movement to raise salaries, and (perhaps not coincidentally) no other National League team offered him a contract.

With the Federal League's Newark Peps, Reulbach put together one last outstanding season in 1915, going 21-10 with a 2.23 ERA.[26] Among that year's highlights were his Opening Day triumph over Chief Bender and his 12-inning win over former Cubs teammate Mordecai Brown. Reulbach also pitched and won the final game in

---

[26] It was, of course, with an inferior league, the Federal League, which included the Chicago Whales or ChiFeds.

Federal League history, defeating the Baltimore Terrapins, 6-0, in the second game of an October 3 doubleheader. The Pittsburgh Pirates acquired the rights to the big right-hander in the Federal League dispersal draft once the league folded but sold him to the Boston Braves just before the start of the 1916 season. Reulbach pitched mostly in relief for the Braves over the next season and a half before ending his career in baseball with Providence of the International League in 1917.

Reulbach's post-baseball years, unfortunately, were not happy ones. He spent a fortune trying to save the life of his constantly ill son, who ended up dying anyway in 1931, and an article in the *Chicago Tribune* the following year referred to Ed at age 50 as a "sad and lonely man."

Considered one of baseball's smartest players during his playing days—(after all, he attended Notre Dame and was attending medical school when the Cubs signed him) teammate Johnny Evers claimed that Ed was "always five years ahead of his time in baseball thought"—Reulbach still devoted much of his time after his career ended to thinking about baseball.

In 1945 he copyrighted the "Leadership Development Plan," under which the then-important position of captain was rotated among all nine players, one inning at a time, as a means of developing leadership qualities. (Maybe that's where the Cubs got their idea of the College of Coaches from – one of the worst ideas in baseball history.) Reulbach died at age 78 on July 17, 1961, in Glens Falls, New York.

 **Ed Reulbach pitching for the Cubs**

# 10 JOE TINKER

Chicago Cubs infielders Joe Tinker, Johnny Evers, and Frank Chance formed the most memorable double-play combination in the history of baseball. Their consistently solid fielding and hitting led the Cubs to four National League pennants (1906-8, 1910) and two World Series wins (1907-8). The Hall of Fame inducted all three simultaneously in 1946. All you need to know about these three Cub players is reflected in the following poem written by sportswriter Franklin Pierce Adams – actually originally from Chicago and a Cub fan - of the *New York Evening Mail* newspaper on July 10, 1910.

These are the saddest of possible words:
"Tinker to Evers to Chance."
Trio of bear cubs, and fleeter than birds,
Tinker  and Evers and Chance.
Ruthlessly pricking our gonfalon bubble,[27]
Making a Giant hit into a double-
Words that are heavy with nothing but trouble:
"Tinker to Evers to Chance."

Joe Tinker

---

[27] A gonfalon is a flag or pennant. In other words, these three players kept the New York team from winning the pennant. And sportswriters were much less objective in those days than they are today. They were cheerleaders for the team in most cases.

Johnny Evers

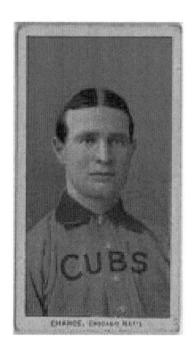

Frank Chance – manager of the Chicago Cubs and described as the Peerless Leader.

The first fellow in the poem – Cubs shortstop Joe Tinker – was a key figure in what was considered the best infield in the league from 1902-12. The Cubs won four pennants and two world championships with Tinker at short, Johnny Evers at second and Frank Chance at first, and as I indicated, the three of them went into the Hall of Fame together in 1946.

They were "linked" in the minds of baseball fans through the ages largely on the strength of the poem, which was about double plays that broke the rallies of opposing teams. While the legend grew from the poem, in reality research has shown that the most double plays the trio ever turned in one season was 58, and not all were started by Tinker. But like all good legends, it's more about the impact on the public than the daily box score. (As they said in *The Man Who Shot Liberty Valance*, when the legend conflicts with the facts, print the legend. Or something like that.)

The son of a contractor, Joseph Bert Tinker was born on July 27, 1880 in Muscotah, Kansas. Joe's twin sister died at an early age, leaving him an only child. When he was two, his family moved to Kansas City where he got his start in baseball at age 14, playing for his school team, the Footpads. (Where do they come up with these mascot names – the Footpads? Sounds like a Dr. Scholl product.) Two years later Joe joined a semipro club called the John Taylors, playing against a future Cub teammate, catcher Johnny Kling of the Schmeltzers. He won a city championship with Hagen's Tailors in 1898, and in June of the following year he left Kansas City and joined a semipro outfit called the Paragons from Parsons, Kansas. After two years of playing semipro baseball, Tinker caught his break when the team owner recommended him to George "White Wings" Tebeau, who was managing Denver of the Western League. Tebeau sold him to Great Falls of the Montana State League in June 1900.[28]

After batting .322 in a combined 57 games for Great Falls and Helena, Tinker played the entire 1901 season for Portland, batting .290 with a league-leading 37 stolen bases for the Pacific Northwest

---

[28] George and his younger brother Patsy were 19th century baseball players.

League champions. Both the Cincinnati Reds and Chicago Orphans were interested in the young third baseman, but Joe requested that he be sold to the Orphans on the advice of outfielder Jack McCarthy, who claimed that he had been treated poorly in his two seasons with the Reds.

At spring training in 1902, new Chicago manager Frank Selee tried out a dozen shortstops in his quest to find a replacement for Barry McCormick, who had jumped to the American League's St. Louis Browns. Ultimately he settled on Tinker, who reluctantly agreed to switch from his preferred position at third base. Joe proved a surprisingly adept hitter, batting .261 as a rookie before reaching a mark of .291 with 70 RBIs in 1903, but he also led all NL shortstops with 72 errors in his first season. His fielding improved dramatically over the next several years, however, and in 1906 he led all NL shortstops with a .944 fielding percentage.[29] Joe went on to lead the league in that category five times, and he also led the NL in range factor four times and double plays twice.

In Joe's fifth season – 1906 - the Cubs won the National League pennant, followed by World Championships in 1907 and 1908, the year of the "Merkle Boner" which gave the Cubs a second chance at the pennant. In the October 8 replay of the game, Tinker's double to center off Christy Mathewson proved to be the pennant-winner, (although the moment was overshadowed by Chance getting assaulted by a crazed fan and suffering broken neck cartilage).

There was an interesting backstage story to the Tinker-Evers-Chance infield, and that was that Tinker and Evers actually didn't speak to each other for many years, except no doubt, for the occasional "I got it!" on pop-ups. Suffice it to say, they worked professionally side-by-side on the infield and didn't reconcile until they shared a radio booth at the 1938 World Series, in which the Cubs played the Yankees. (And the Cubs lost, of course.) But that story was not really true, as you will see in a moment.

---

[29] Fielding percentages in those days were nowhere what they are today, probably in large part because of the quality of baseball fields and better gloves.

Tinker played with the Cubs through the 1912 season – he did not want to play for new Cub manager Johnny Evers after 1912 - and was then traded to the Reds in 1913 where he was player/manager, and then repeated the dual function with the short-lived Federal League team in Chicago.

When the Federal League folded after the 1915 season, Whales owner Charles Weeghman purchased the Cubs and brought Tinker with him as manager. Joe lasted only one season, leading his old team to a fifth-place finish. In 1917 he became part owner and manager of the Columbus team in the American Association. Due to his wife's health problems, Joe sold his interest in the team in 1920 and moved to Orlando where he became owner-manager of the Orlando Gulls of the Florida State League. He became one of Orlando's leading citizens, investing in real estate and building a racetrack, dog track, and ballpark. But Tinker lost his wealth during the Great Depression.

In his remaining years he worked as a scout for the Cubs and operated a successful billiard room in Orlando. He also worked as a boiler inspector at the Orlando air force base during World War II. Despite the rumors that he and Evers did not speak to each other until the 1938 World Series, they apparently went on a ten-week theatrical tour in 1929 to perform a skit – obviously they spoke to one another in order to perform the skit, unless it was a pantomime.

Joe suffered from diabetes in his later years but lived long enough to enjoy his election into the National Baseball Hall of Fame in 1946. Joe Tinker passed away in Orlando on his 68th birthday, July 27, 1948, the last of the famed trio of bear cubs to die. He is the namesake of Tinker Field, which remained the home of minor-league baseball in Orlando, Florida until 2000.

# 11 JOHNNY EVERS

**Johnny Evers, all 125 pounds of him**

The typical contemporary baseball fan might look at Johnny Evers' lifetime batting average of .270 and conclude that Evers' Hall of Fame credentials are fraudulent, and that he rode into Cooperstown on the coat tails of some catchy baseball verse by Franklin P. Adams with the refrain "Tinker to Evers to Chance." The poem did achieve a bit of fame and is still referenced regularly, but Evers was not dependent on it for his Hall of Fame status. Nor was his reputation made solely by the infamous Merkle incident, although it certainly enhanced his status. No, Johnny Evers in his day was simply considered a great baseball player, the heart and soul of the great Chicago Cubs teams of the period, a player who was entirely deserving of baseball's highest accolades.

One important thing forgotten by most of Evers' detractors is that Evers played in the dead ball era when pitching dominated hitting. In 1908 when Evers hit .300, that figure was good for fifth best in the National League. By contrast, 2.03 was the highest ERA among the

Cubs' top four pitchers: Three-fingered Brown (29-9), Ed Reulbach (24-7), Jake Pfiester (12-10), and Orval Overall (15-11). Evers never put up any gaudy offensive numbers, but he was a nuisance at the plate; a fact indicated by his also finishing in the Top Five in the league in 1908 in runs, bases on balls, and stolen bases. His highest average came in 1912 when he batted .341, good for fourth in the NL.

Evers' bat was the least significant part of his game. In an era when each and every run was fought for, defense was far more important than it is today (even though fielding percentages don't show it because of fields that pale in comparison to the fields of today and poor gloves, as I have mentioned); and Evers was not only the best fielder at his position, but also an innovator. Experts credit Johnny with popularizing sweep tags, catching throws one-handed, making side-armed snap throws, and moving out of the way of sliding runners – moves that are routinely used by all second basemen today.

Most important of all and the key to Evers' career was his personality, a huge complex persona that dwarfed his small physical stature. Evers was driven to succeed and to win as few major leaguers have ever been, before or since. He was a feisty baseball player who battled opponents, umpires, and even teammates like shortstop Joe Tinker constantly. His desire to win was unequaled, and he assembled a record of winning that may be unparalleled in baseball history. The Cubs won four pennants (in 1906, 07, 08, 10), with Evers manning second base, and, with the Boston Braves, another pennant in 1914. In his 15-year career, from 1903 through 1917, the teams Evers played for never finished worse than third place, a record that even Babe Ruth cannot match (with either the Red Sox or Yankees).

Evers always had trouble controlling this intensity and his temper. One expert even compared his behavior to that of The Three Stooges. Some experts liken him to that prototypical player whom you hate when he is on the other team but love when he becomes a teammate – think of A.J. Pierzynski in more recent times. His battles with teammate Joe Tinker are well known but probably exaggerated.

**Anyone who is compared to my favorite comedy team – The Three Stooges – can't be all bad, after all. Nyuk, Nyuk!**[30]

An excellent bunter, accomplished base stealer, and pesky left-handed hitter who usually had the National League's best walk-to-strikeout ratio after his first few seasons, Johnny Evers was considered one of the Deadball Era's smartest and best all-around players, but he was just as well known for his fiery disposition.

One would guess that his nickname, "The Human Crab," was given to him because of his less-than-sunny disposition, but one would be wrong. Evers was originally given the name due to his unorthodox manner of sidling over to ground balls before gobbling them up, but most baseball fans eventually considered it better suited to his temperament than his fielding. A 5'9", 125 lb. dervish with a protruding jaw that came to be a symbol of the man (it seemed like he was always jawing about something), Evers developed a reputation as a troublemaker by squabbling regularly with teammates, opponents, and especially umpires. "They claim he is a crab, and perhaps they are right," said Cleveland Indians manager Joe Birmingham. "But I would like to have 25 such crabs playing for me. If I did, I would have no doubts over the pennant. They would win hands down."

---

[30] Actually, I like the Marx Brothers and Three Stooges equally.

John Joseph Evers was born on July 21, 1881, in Troy, New York. His father was a saloon keeper, and most of his relatives played sandlot baseball. Johnny tipped the scales at just 100 lbs. when he signed with his hometown Troy club in the New York State League early in the 1902 season. When he appeared in a game at nearby Albany the fans reportedly assumed that he was some sort of comic act – sort of an early version of the San Diego Chicken, I guess - but the 20-year-old shortstop fielded everything hit his way and won the game with a three-run double.

**San Diego Chicken and Friends**

Later that summer the manager of the Chicago Cubs, Frank Selee, heard about a pitcher named Alex Hardy who was pitching for the Troy team. He arranged an exhibition between his club and the Trojans, a common practice at the time. Hardy was impressive, so Selee offered the Troy ownership $1,000 for him. Hardy's employers countered by requesting $1,500, claiming that another major-league club was willing to shell out that amount. "I'll tell you what I'll do," Selee responded. "If you throw in that kid who played short today, I'll give you the $1,500." The owners of the Troy team were quick to oblige. Evers was batting .285 and leading the New York State League with 10 home runs (only two fewer than he hit in his entire

18-year major-league career), but he was regarded as a nuisance because of his short temper and his insistence that the local ballpark be available for practice at all times of the day. He also committed plenty of errors at short, though he had great range in the field.[31]

Making his major-league debut on September 1, 1902, Johnny played his customary position while Selee moved his regular shortstop, fellow rookie Joe Tinker, to third base.[32] Three days later, however, Selee rearranged the infield, moving Evers to second and returning Tinker to short, the positions at which they remained for the next decade. Despite occasional flashes of brilliance, Evers' 26-game trial during the final month of that season was a bust; his defense was inconsistent and he batted .222 without a single extra-base hit, drawing just three walks and stealing only a single base. But regular second-baseman Bobby Lowe suffered a severe knee injury late in 1902, and by spring training the following year it still hadn't healed properly. Evers won the starting job by default. This time he was ready, batting .293, stealing 25 bases, and contributing solid defense. Lowe never played another game for the Cubs after that.

Over the next ten years, the mutual antipathy between Evers and his keystone partner, Tinker, was legendary although perhaps overstated. They didn't speak to each other off the field for more than three decades. Some commentators dated their animosity to a highly publicized on-field brawl in 1905, but years later Evers told a different story. "One day early in 1907, he threw me a hard ball; it wasn't any farther than from here to there," Evers claimed, pointing to a lamp about 10 feet from where he sat. "It was a real hard ball, like a catcher throwing to second." The throw bent back one of the fingers on Evers' right hand. "I yelled to him, you so-and-so. He laughed. That's the last word we had for-well, I just don't know how

---

[31] Alex Hardy had a lifetime record of 3-3, all with the Cubs, while Evers is in the baseball Hall of Fame. I wish the Cubs had made more deals like that one instead of Brock for Broglio. There I go again!

[32] A great trivia question is "Who was the third baseman for all those great Cub teams?" The answer – Harry Steinfeldt.

long." Whatever the reason for their bitterness, Evers and Tinker were an impeccable defensive tandem on the diamond. "Tinker and myself hated each other," Evers admitted, "but we loved the Cubs. We wouldn't fight for each other, but we'd come close to killing people for our team. That was one of the answers to the Cubs' success." The Cubs should have had more players like these two guys over the years.

Evers didn't hit his first major-league home run until July 21, 1905, when he lifted a Chick Fraser pitch over the fence in the right-field corner at Boston's South End Grounds.[33] By that point he had already appeared in more than 350 big-league games. But Johnny made up for his lack of power with his mastery of the overall game. In 1906 he stole a career-high 49 bases, and the next year he pilfered 46. Evers also generally increased his bases on balls each season, peaking at 108 in 1910, only eight behind league-leader Miller Huggins. "I am convinced that in my own career I could usually have hit 30 points higher if I had made a specialty of hitting," said Evers about his a lifetime batting average of .270. "Some lumbering bonehead who does make a specialty of hitting and nothing else may forge well across the .300 line and everybody says, 'What a grand hitter.' The fact is, the bonehead may have been playing rotten baseball when he got that average and someone else who didn't look to be in his class might be the better hitter of the two. Of course there are plenty of times when there is nothing like the old single. But there are plenty of other times when the batter at the plate should focus his attention on trying to fool the pitcher. In my own case I have frequently faced the pitcher when I had no desire whatever to hit. I wanted to get a base on balls."

Evers was a decent enough hitter. He batted an even .300 in 1908, the first of only two times in his career that he reached that magical number. He also played a crucial role in that year's pennant race, the closest and most exciting in baseball history. On September 4 the Cubs were locked in a scoreless duel in Pittsburgh when the Pirates loaded the bases with two outs in the bottom of the ninth. On what

---

[33] Remember, that's the Boston Braves, not the Boston Red Sox

appeared to be a game-winning hit to center, the runner at first, Warren Gill, left the field without bothering to touch second base. Evers, standing on second, called for the ball and demanded that umpire Hank O'Day rule the play a forceout, which would nullify the run and send the game into extra innings. Gill's maneuver was customary in those days, and O'Day refused to make the call that Evers was seeking. "That night O'Day came to look me up, which was an unusual thing in itself," Evers recalled many years later. "Sitting in a corner in the lobby, he told me that he wanted to discuss the play. O'Day then agreed that my play was legal and that under the circumstances, a runner coming down from first and not touching second on the final base hit was out." Evers' account may not be trustworthy, especially given O'Day's exceptionally reclusive nature and the lengthy period between the event and the retelling, but the incident undoubtedly had a pronounced effect on the umpire, as was demonstrated by subsequent events – the Merkle play, to be specific.

An almost identical situation arose on September 23, this time with the Cubs battling the Giants at the Polo Grounds. When New York's Al Bridwell hit an apparent game-winning single with two outs in the bottom of the ninth, the runner on first, Fred Merkle, headed for the clubhouse without touching second. Evers called for the ball, eventually got one (though probably not the ball Bridwell hit), and stepped on second base. O'Day was again the umpire, and this time he called the runner out. Given the irregularity of the call, the critical nature of the game, the temperaments of the opposing managers, and the animosity between the Cubs and Giants – fierce rivals and the two best teams in the league, although the Pirates were right up there also - O'Day's verdict sparked a firestorm of controversy. Eventually NL president Harry Pulliam ruled the game a tie, to be replayed if it had any impact on the pennant race. It did.

The Cubs went back to New York for a one-game playoff, winning 4-2 to secure their third consecutive NL pennant, and went on to beat the Tigers in the World Series for the second straight year, with Evers batting .350 and leading all players on both teams with five runs scored. Evers' headiness on the play that became known as "Merkle's Boner" was given due credit for the Cubs' win and cemented his reputation as one of the smartest players in baseball.

Evers lived for baseball, and his complete devotion to the game took its toll in numerous ways: a failed marriage, bankrupt businesses, and a nervous breakdown. He came back from the nervous breakdown in 1914 to lead the Braves, along with Rabbit Maranville, to one of the most unlikely pennants and World Series championships in baseball history; a triumph that settled once and for all his claim to greatness among his contemporaries. His knowledge of the game and his leadership were so valued that after he could no longer play, his services as a coach, manager, or scout were always in demand.

Evers was married to Helen Fitzgibbons. His son, John J. Evers, Jr., served as a Lieutenant in World War II, assigned to the Pacific Theater of Operations. When his son was 11 years old, Evers bought part of the Albany Senators and gave him the stock.

## Life after Baseball

Evers operated a sporting goods store in Albany, New York in 1923. However, Evers lost his money and filed for bankruptcy in 1936. The store was passed down to Evers' descendants. He also worked as superintendent of Bleecker Stadium in Albany and spent time teaching baseball to sandlot players.

Evers suffered a stroke in August 1942, which paralyzed the right side of his body. He remained bedridden or confined to a wheelchair for most of the next five years. Evers died of a cerebral hemorrhage in 1947 at St. Peter's Hospital in Albany.

Evers' election to the Hall of Fame a year before his death in 1947 was in no way controversial but seen as mere justice for a most deserving candidate.

One of the smartest players in baseball history, no question about that. Johnny Evers.

**The great Johnny Evers, choking up on the bat**

# 12 FRANK CHANCE – THE PEERLESS LEADER

Few men in the history of baseball have seen great success as both a player and as a manager. One or the other, yes, but not both. Frank Chance was one of them.

"He was a great player – I think one of the best first basemen ever in the game – but in addition he was a great leader because he asked no man to take any chance that he would not take himself and because he had the power to instill enthusiasm even in a losing cause," said fellow Hall of Fame manager John McGraw.

Born in Fresno, California, on September 9, 1876, Frank Leroy Chance did not play any true form of organized baseball until his college years at the University of California, where he was pursuing an education in dentistry. It was while playing in an independent league in summer 1897, after transferring to Washington College in Irvington, California, that the right-handed hitter caught the attention of Cubs outfielder and fellow Californian Bill Lange. (Lange was still with the team in 1897.) Lange convinced Cubs management to sign

Chance, sight unseen, as a backup catcher and outfielder, and he joined the team in the early spring of 1898. He made an immediate impact his rookie season, batting .279 with 32 runs scored and 14 runs batted in while playing in just 53 games in the majors (he also hit his first of only 20 career home runs, off Washington Senators pitcher Cy Swaim.).

Chance continued his role as a reserve catcher through the 1902 season, always batting slightly below .300 and never playing in over 76 games. This was due primarily to his numerous broken fingers and frequent hand injuries suffered while attempting to corral foul tipped balls. In 1903, when Johnny Kling, one of the best catchers of the era, took over the full responsibilities behind the plate for the Cubs,[34] and regular first baseman Bill Hanlon unexpectedly abandoned the team, manager Frank Selee moved Chance to first base as a temporary replacement until a more suitable fielder could be found. (What a great move!) Chance, incensed by being assigned yet another position, threatened retirement but a pay raise helped to mollify any hard feelings. Regardless, the change suited Chance perfectly, as he played in over 100 games (125) and batted over .300 (.327) for the first time in his career. In addition, it was in 1903 that Chance first made his presence known on the base paths while stealing a National League leading 67 bases, still the most ever for a Chicago Cub player in the modern era. (Post 1900 is considered the modern era.)

When Selee fell seriously ill in midseason 1905, Frank "Husk" Chance, so named because of his husky physical stature (6'0", 190 lbs.), was named manager and led a strong, yet unmotivated Cubs team from National League mediocrity to a third-place finish. Meanwhile, Chance hit .316 with 92 runs scored and 70 runs batted in.

The Cubs, now owned by Charles Webb Murphy, retained Chance as both manager and player for the 1906 season. That season was the turning point for the Cubs as the team finished first with a record of

---

[34] Kling was the Cubs' regular catcher from 1901-1910 and had a lifetime average of .271. He might be the 2nd or 3rd best catcher in Cub history.

116-36 and a winning percentage of .763 that has never been equaled. Individually, Chance had a career season, batting .319 and leading the National League in both runs (103) and stolen bases (57). Although the heavily favored Cubs lost the 1906 "Crosstown Classic" World Series to their Southside rivals, the Chicago White Sox, Chance would lead them back to win the World Series in 1907, defeating the Detroit Tigers four games to none; and in 1908, defeating the Tigers again, this time by the count of four games to one. In 1910, Chance's Cubs were back in the World Series, although they lost that series to the Philadelphia Athletics in five games. Chance fared much better as a Cubs manager than he ever did as a Cubs player, winning 100 games four out of seven full seasons (not including the 1905 season when he took over for Frank Selee) and never finishing lower than third place in the National League.

Throughout his managerial career, however, Chance displayed an infamous lack of good sportsmanship that would make the notorious Ty Cobb blush – certainly more common in those days than today. Chance once incited a riot at the Polo Grounds after physically assaulting New York Giants pitcher Joe McGinnity, and on more than one occasion tossed beer bottles at fans in Brooklyn when he felt they were being too unruly, or perhaps not unruly enough. For his fighting prowess (he spent several off-seasons working as a prizefighter), old-school boxing legends Jim Corbett and John L. Sullivan both called Chance "the greatest amateur brawler of all time." Interestingly, he made outfielder Solly Hofman postpone his own wedding until the off-season, fearing that too much marital bliss might affect Hofman's playing ability.

It was reported that Chance would fine his own players for shaking hands with opposing players, win or lose, and had no qualms about releasing players for failing to meet his demands to the letter.[35] Chance once remarked, "You do things my way or you meet me after the game." Generally, his players complied, and it is no small wonder that he earned the nickname, "The Peerless Leader," since he was

---

[35] Dealing with players on the opposing team was quite different in those days, before players became unionized and engaged in collective bargaining. They are now good buddies instead of enemies.

simultaneously respected and disliked by those who played for him, with him, and against him.

Plagued by injuries for a great deal of his career, most notably injured by a barrage of beanings[36] due to his propensity for crowding the plate, Chance's playing career was cut relatively short. By 1911, he had virtually phased himself out of the everyday lineup, playing in only 31 games over the course of the season. He had completely lost his hearing in one ear and partially lost it in the other, causing him to unintentionally talk in an annoyingly whiney tone. As if that weren't bad enough, he had also developed blood clots in his brain from the beanings. Incredibly, he was released by the Cubs as both a player and a manager while hospitalized for brain surgery in 1912 after a heated hospital room argument with Cubs owner Murphy over Murphy's releasing good players to save the team money.

Making a miraculous recovery from his brain injuries, Chance spent the 1913 and 1914 seasons as a player-manager for the hapless American League New York Yankees[37] (resigning late in the 1914 season), yet did not play in more than 12 games in either of the two seasons. He hung up his major league spikes temporarily to return home to California, where he operated an orange grove, and briefly owned and managed the Los Angeles team of the Pacific Coast League. He returned for a short stint in the major leagues in 1923 as a manager for the Boston Red Sox. The Red Sox finished dead last in the American League that year, and the following season Chance accepted the job as manager of his old crosstown nemesis, the Chicago White Sox, drawing the ire of Cub fans for such an act of treason. However, Chance's health took an unexpected turn for the worse, precluding him taking the job. He was ill for several months and he died on September 15, 1924 at the age of only 48.

---

[36] Today they would be called concussions and taken much more seriously by the team than they were then.

[37] The Yankees did not make their first world series appearance until 1921. Since then they have made a total of 40 World Series appearances. But in the early 1900's, they were doormats.

With his .664 winning percentage as manager of the Cubs, he is clearly the franchise's best all-time manager. (Can you imagine a Cub manager with a .664 winning percentage? I hope Joe Maddon is as lucky.) For his overall managing career, he posted a record of 946-648 for a winning percentage of .593. As a player, Chance is the Cubs' all-time career stolen base leader with 402; led the team in batting average in 1903, 1904, 1905 and 1907; and batted .300, with 21 hits, 11 runs, and 10 stolen bases in four World Series.

One can only wonder what kind of numbers Chance would have put up as a player had he avoided injury or had the training, rehabilitation, and medical facilities that today's players have at their disposal. Frank Chance was rewarded for his contributions to the game of baseball, both as a player and a manager, in 1946 when he was inducted into the National Baseball Hall of Fame in Cooperstown, New York, by the Committee on Baseball Veterans. Honored in the same class were former teammates Joe Tinker and Johnny Evers. The Trio of Bear Cubs lives on!

**1910 photo of Frank Chance taken by New York freelance photographer Paul Thompson. Now HE looks like a manager!**

# 13 JAMES (HIPPO) VAUGHN

While the Chicago Cubs have had a number of great right-handed pitchers throughout their existence, the number of really outstanding lefties has been small.

Without doubt, James (Hippo) Vaughn is the greatest left-handed pitcher in Chicago Cub history. Vaughn had 178 lifetime victories, and 151 of them came with the North Siders. (Larry French, with 95 victories, has the second-most wins of any Cub lefty.) He had five 20-win seasons for the North Siders during his peak years. Moreover, Vaughn was involved in probably the greatest pitching performance ever by two pitchers in the same game – a double no-hitter by Vaughn and Fred Toney of the Cincinnati Reds on May 2, 1917.

James Leslie Vaughn was a Texas-size pitcher worthy of the Lone Star State. At 6' 4" and 215 pounds, James Leslie Vaughn must have intimidated many of the small-framed players of the dead ball era. Later in his career he was reported to have ballooned to almost 300 pounds – more likely around 230 for most of his career. But Vaughn was not named because of his weight or likeness to a hippopotamus, but for the ungainly way he carried his frame when he ran- a slow, side-to-side lumbering gate that apparently reminded someone of a hippopotamus. (Frankly, all the hippos I have ever seen have been IN the water, not walking around outside, except for one time at the Brookfield Zoo in Chicago, when I was a little tyke.).

Born April 9, 1888, in Weatherford, Texas, due west of Fort Worth, Jim was one of eight children of Josephine and Thomas Vaughn, a stonemason. Finishing school in Weatherford, he began pitching professionally with Temple in the Texas League in 1906. He spent 1907 at Corsicana in the North Texas League, then moved on to Hot Springs in the Arkansas State League, going 9-1 and getting a shot with the New York Highlanders (Yankees). He debuted with New York on June 19, 1908. James was a bit wild for the Highlanders, and finished the season with Scranton of the New York State League, his 2-4 record offset by six complete games, a shutout, and a fine 2.39 ERA. Vaughn began 1909 with Macon in the South Atlantic League, where he threw a no-hitter, had a 1.95 ERA, suffered little run support, and wound up 9-16. He moved to Louisville in the American Association that same year, threw another no-hitter, and went 8-1 with an ERA of 2.05.

Vaughn rejoined the Highlanders at spring training in 1910 and so impressed manager George Stallings that he gave Vaughn the opening day assignment. Thus he became the youngest pitcher ever to start an opening day game for the Yankees. Vaughn faced the Boston Red Sox and Eddie Cicotte[38] on April 14 at Hilltop Park. After a rough start in which he gave up three runs in the first three innings and another in the fifth, Vaughn settled down, and he and Joe Wood (relieving Cicotte) pitched shutout ball until the game was called on account of darkness after 14 innings with the score tied 4-4. The game was certainly an indication of good things to come for Vaughn. Overshadowed only by Russ Ford's brilliant rookie season of 26-6 with a 1.65 ERA, Vaughn went 13-11 for the season with an excellent 1.83 ERA, 18 complete games, and five shutouts.

---

[38] Ed Cicotte was the key pitcher involved in the Black Sox scandal for the 1919 White Sox.

Hal Chase became manager of the Highlanders late in 1910 and returned for the full 1911 season. Chase, like Stallings before him, was impressed with Vaughn and selected him for the April 12 opener in Philadelphia against Chief Bender. Both men pitched great, with Vaughn winning a 2-1 decision and helping himself with a single. The rest of the season was a disappointment, however, as Vaughn finished up 8-10 with a 4.39 ERA.

Vaughn got into the opener in New York on April 12, 1912, against Boston and Joe Wood, recording the last two outs in the ninth inning after Ray Caldwell surrendered four runs, giving Boston a 5-3 win. From that point on, Vaughn was 2-8 with an ERA of 5.14 and a shutout, until June 26, when New York sold him to Washington for the waiver price. He did better in Washington, going 4-3 with a 2.89 ERA. Washington sold him to Kansas City of the (minor league) American Association, where he finished the 1912 season poorly, 2-3 while giving up over five runs a game. Frankly, he looked like nothing special at this point in time.

In 1913 with Kansas City of the American Association, Vaughn went 20-13. Toward the end of the season, the Cubs took a chance on him that paid off immediately. He finished the season 5-1 with six complete games, two shutouts, and an ERA of 1.45. Sometimes a player, a team, and a city come together almost magically. That certainly was the case with Hippo Vaughn, the Cubs, and Chicago. He had found a home.

Vaughn's 1914 season was pretty much a carbon copy of what the next six seasons would be: 21-13 with a 2.05 ERA. Indeed, looking at Vaughn's numbers during this period is like looking at a lefty pitcher like Warren Spahn's career over any half-dozen years - 17 to 23 wins, a high percentage of complete games, 260 to 300 innings pitched, good control, a decent number of strikeouts, and an ERA below the league average. Of course, Spahn did it more than twice as long. Vaughn's 1915 record was a bit off, 20-12 but with an ERA of 2.87 that was the worst of his prime years and the only season that he had fewer complete games (18) than wins. He slipped to 17-15 in 1916 but brought his ERA down to 2.20. As further proof of his consistency, he pitched four shutouts each season.

The 1918 season was particularly memorable for Hippo Vaughn and the Cubs. The season was shortened to 140 games and ended on September 2 as the government enacted a "Fight or Work" decree in support of the war effort for World War I. Vaughn tailed off a bit as the season wound down, but his exceptional work had propelled the Cubs to the pennant 10.5 games ahead of the Giants. Vaughn captured the pitchers' Triple Crown, leading the National League in wins with 22 (against just 10 losses), strikeouts with 148, and ERA at 1.74. Equally impressive were his eight shutouts, which stood as the National League record for southpaws (tied with Lefty Leifield of Pittsburgh in 1906 and teammate Lefty Tyler in 1918) until Carl Hubbell threw 10 in 1933.

Vaughn didn't let up in the Series against the Red Sox, but he had little luck against three excellent pitchers. Fellow lefty Babe Ruth – yes, Ruth was a pitcher early in his career before the Red Sox traded him to the Yankees in even a worse trade than the Brock for Broglio trade - beat Vaughn, 1-0, in Game One. Carl Mays, who would win over two hundred games in his career, took Game Three from Vaughn, 2-1[39]. Vaughn then shut out another two-hundred-game winner, Sad Sam Jones, 3-0, in Game Five – not the same Sad Same Jones who pitched for the Cubs in the 1950's, by the way. His brilliant work included three complete games, three earned runs, an ERA of 1.00-and a 1-2 record. The Cubs lost the Series in six games.

Vaughn essentially duplicated his 1918 effort the next season, going 21-14 with 141 strikeouts, his usual four shutouts, and a 1.79 ERA in 1919. The Cubs, however, went 75-65 and slipped to third place. In hindsight, the 1920 season showed some signs that not all was well. The Cubs continued to decline, going 75-79 and finishing fifth, so Vaughn's 19-16 record looked good in comparison. However, his ERA was a high (for him) 2.54, though near his career ERA of 2.49.

---

[39] Carl Mays is best remembered for throwing the pitch that hit Cleveland shortstop Ray Chapman in the head and led to his untimely death in August of 1920. But he also had a career record of 207-126 and a 2.92 ERA over fifteen seasons, and remains one of the best pitchers not honored in the Hall of Fame. Chapman is still the only major leaguer to die on the field from a pitched baseball.

His strikeouts fell to 131, slightly off his usual performance. What might have raised alarms was Vaughn's giving up 301 hits in 301 innings, the first time he had surrendered a hit an inning since 1912. Nevertheless, no one thought the end was near.

However, his major league career ended abruptly in 1921 amidst a flurry of mystery and drama. On July 9, he took the mound in the Polo Grounds with a dismal 3-10 record. In the fourth inning he surrendered a grand slam homer to Giants catcher Frank Snyder. Even more insulting, pitcher Phil Douglas followed with his first career home run. Cub manager Johnny Evers then gave Vaughn the hook. Two days later, Vaughn was nowhere to be found and the Cubs announced that Vaughn would be suspended if and when he returned to the team. Whether because of injury, weight gain, or age, Vaughn had suddenly lost his stuff.

By early August, Vaughn was still AWOL and the Cubs reportedly suspended him for what the *Chicago Tribune* described as "failure to keep in fighting trim." Furthermore, Vaughn had allegedly signed a contract to play for the Beloit Fairies, a non-affiliated team owned by the Fairbanks Morse Engine Company who manufactured everything from typewriters to locomotives – things were much different in those days as far as a player's status. A Hippo as a member of the Fairies sounds like something out of Disney's *Fantasia*.

When Evers was suddenly fired as manager, his replacement, Bill Killefer, and Cubs president Bill Veeck Sr. agreed to reinstate Vaughn if Commissioner Landis agreed. Landis, however, decided to suspend Vaughn for the rest of the season for signing the contract with Beloit. Vaughn never returned to the Cubs or the major leagues again. Various reports list assorted reasons for his departure. 1. He was fed up with Evers. 2. He had a sore arm. 3. His weight had finally affected his performance.

But Vaughn kept the reason or reasons to himself. His new career in semi-pro ball lasted another sixteen years and he finally hung up his mitt at age 49. Away from baseball, he was an assembler for a refrigeration products company.

Vaughn died in Chicago in 1966. At the time of his death, he still had bragging rights as the Cubs all-time leader in wins by a left-handed pitcher with 151 victories. As of this writing, that distinction still belongs to the man called Hippo. And Frankly, I don't think that signing Jon Lester – in his 30s – or anyone on the current Cub roster - is going to change that.

## The Double No Hitter

It was an extremely chilly day in Chicago at Weegham Park (Wrigley Field) on May 2, 1917 – wow, what a surprise – a chilly day in May in Chicago. Just around 3,500 fans showed up to watch what would appear to have been just another baseball game. The Cincinnati Reds were in town to play the Cubs.

The Reds had 29-year-old Fred Toney on the mound. Toney had a great fastball and was a solid pitcher who had won 17 and 14 games in the two previous seasons. Toney won 139 games in his major league career. Hippo Vaughn was on the mound for the Chicago Cubs.

One other interesting fact: In 1909, eight years before the game in question, Fred Toney had pitched one of the most incredible games in minor league history. Fred had pitched a 17-inning no-hitter for his Winchester, Kentucky, team in the Bluegrass League. This would appear to be the longest no-hitter in any known baseball league and was definitely an eerie precursor to what was about to take place.

Reds manager Christy Mathewson put an all-right-handed lineup against Hippo Vaughn, hoping to help his team against the tough left-hander. Nonetheless, Hippo got out of the gate in superb fashion, retiring the first nine Reds batters in a row.

The Reds' Heinie Groh – yes, they used nicknames like Heinie, as in Heinie Manush and Heinie Zimmerman in those days - led off the fourth inning with a walk, but was thrown out stealing. Gus Getz then walked, but was erased on a double play. These would be the only Reds to reach first base after nine innings.

Fred Toney was just as unhittable, issuing just two walks, both to the Cubs' Cy Williams, in the second and fifth innings.

According to the estimated calculations, the odds of a no-hitter being pitched in a Major League baseball game are 13,000 to one. And there has been only one double no-hitter in 140 years of major league baseball. As the small crowd sat in astonishment in the stands, and the Reds and the Cubs sat and watched and shook their heads in wonder, everyone present realized that they had watched one of the strangest games in baseball history, something completely unprecedented - a double no-hitter for nine innings.

In the top of the tenth inning, Hippo Vaughn retired the lead-off hitter, Gus Getz, popping out to the catcher. But then things began to unravel. Reds shortstop Larry Kopf hit a single, breaking the spell. Earle "Greasy" Neal – I have to admit that Greasy was not a common nickname, even in those days - hit a fly ball to outfielder Cy Williams for out number two. Then outfielder Cy Williams dropped a fly ball hit by Hal Chase – the same Hal Chase who managed Vaughn in 1910 and 1911 - putting runners on second and third.

Jim Thorpe

**The great Jim Thorpe, who participated in that game**

The next batter was the legendary athlete Jim Thorpe, who had won gold medals five years previously at the 1912 Olympics in Stockholm. Thorpe hit a ball right back to Vaughn, who threw the ball to his catcher Art Wilson. (It is often asked, since the ball was hit right back to him, why didn't Hippo just throw the ball to first base to nail Jim Thorpe? But Hippo said he knew "Thorpe ran like a racehorse," so he threw the ball to home instead.)[40]

The ball hit Wilson in the chest protector as Kopf ran across the plate and scored the game's first run. According to Vaughn, "Now some say Wilson wasn't expecting the throw. The truth is that Art just went paralyzed. Just stood there with his hands at his sides staring at me."

Hal Chase saw the frozen catcher and started tearing toward home plate, too. Vaughn said to Wilson, "Are you going to let him score, too?" Wilson snapped out of his daze and tagged Chase out at the plate easily, ending the inning.

In the bottom of the tenth, Fred Toney retired the last three Cubs in order, preserving his own no-hitter. Cy Williams, who had had two walks that day, ended the game, striking out on a 3 and 2 pitch.

Cub catcher Art Wilson apologized to his pitcher in the Cubs clubhouse. Hippo Vaughn remembered "Wilson cried like a baby after the game. He grabbed my hand and said, 'I just went out on you, Jim, I just went tight.'" "But I wasn't sore," said Vaughn. "I just lost another ballgame, that's all."

What should we remember about Hippy Vaughn? Three things come immediately to mind:

---

[40] Jim Thorpe was played in the movies by Burt Lancaster, one of my all-time favorite movie stars, in the film *Jim Thorpe, All American.* Lancaster was chosen for the part, not because he looked like a Native American, but because he was also an outstanding athlete. Burt got his start as a circus trapeze artist before becoming an actor. If you don't believe me, just watch *The Crimson Pirate* some time.

1. He threw hard, had good control, gave up less than a hit an inning, and was stingy with runs.

2. His 151 wins as a Cub is miles ahead of Larry French's 95. He won twenty games five times in seven years.

3. No other Cub southpaw won 20 games more than twice (Jake Weimer in 1903 and 1904). No Cub lefty achieved it after Vaughn in 1919 until Dick Ellsworth did so in 1963. No one's done it since.

Vaughn was simply an excellent Cub pitcher for seven years and a great one for some of that time, but except for one day in May of 1917, he's pretty much forgotten. That is a shame.

 **Hippo Vaughn on the mound**

# 14 THE MILLION DOLLAR OUTFIELD

The Cubs have had some great outfields throughout their existence, but none quite like what I am calling the Million Dollar Outfield.

In the late 1920's through early 1930's, Riggs Stephenson, Kiki Cuyler, and Hack Wilson formed the greatest outfield in the National League. They all played with other teams in their careers, but all three had far and away their best years with the Cubs. They helped lead the Cubs to National League pennants in 1929 and 1932 – no World Series championships, of course – but their outstanding offensive contributions led them to be recognized as the Million Dollar Outfield. Moreover, in the Cubs' 1929 pennant-winning year, Stephenson combined with Hall of Famers Hack Wilson and Kiki Cuyler as the only outfield in NL history in which each member had more than 100 RBI. (Stephenson 110, Wilson 159, Cuyler 102). That's a total of 371 RBI's from the outfield alone!

**Left to right – Riggs Stephenson, Hack Wilson, and Kiki Cuyler**

### Jackson (Riggs) Stephenson
The left fielder in that group – and the only non-Hall of Famer - was

Riggs Stephenson, the pride of Akron, Alabama. Stephenson's lifetime batting average of .336 was 22nd best of all time. [41]

The Riggs Stephenson story is generally told as one of "what might have been." Born in Akron, Alabama on January 5, 1898, Stephenson attended his home state university, the University of Alabama, and according to his standard narrative, Stephenson suffered a shoulder injury incurred while playing football at Alabama; as a result, he was unable to make long throws, which affected his playing baseball and led to a shorter career than he might have had otherwise. While Stephenson played sports with the Crimson Tide, he was apparently also a decent, clean-living fellow. Dr. George Denny, president of the university, said of him: "He is the embodiment of cleanliness, manliness, and courage."[42]

Stephenson quit school at Alabama and immediately made the jump to professional baseball, where he signed with the defending World Series champion Cleveland Indians in 1921 at the age of 23. Riggs was one of those guys who went straight from college to the big

---

[41] And that included a number of players who played before 1900, when batting averages tended to be inflated.

[42] www.bleedcubbieblue.com

leagues (Ernie Banks was another who never played in the minor leagues per se.). During his early career with Cleveland, he was a second baseman, where his suspect arm made it difficult for him to turn double plays. As a result, he saw limited playing time, averaging only 66 games per season during his five years in Cleveland.

Stephenson made his major league debut on April 13, 1921, and continued to play sparingly during the remainder of the season. His weak arm and throwing difficulties weakened his fielding abilities at second base, as seen by the 17 errors he committed in the 54 games he played at the position that season. However, Riggs' hitting compensated for his fielding woes; he hit 17 doubles among his 68 hits during his 65-game season that year. Stephenson batted .330, reaching a mark that he would frequently surpass during the rest of his professional career. He was acquired by the Cubs in 1926, another great move by the team. (Where were these front office guys when the Cubs traded Brock for Broglio? I know, I am starting to sound like a broken record. But that trade scarred me for life!)

But with the Cubs, Riggs Stephenson was converted to a serviceable defensive left fielder, although his shoulder still limited his ability to throw out runners. In nine seasons, he averaged 109 games per season. While he did have markedly fewer outfield assists than either of his partners in the Cubs' outfield (Kiki Cuyler and Hack Wilson), he still averaged over 10 per 154-game season, comparable to most modern-day left fielders.

Regardless of whether his defense is properly described as "suspect" or "serviceable," Stephenson's offense was excellent. He led the National League in doubles in 1927, and he batted worse than .319 only once, in 1934, his last season with the Cubs, when injuries had finally caught up with him. He was instrumental in two Cubs World Series runs (1929 and 1932), achieving a .378/.410/.432 line, scoring five runs, and racking up seven RBIs over the course of the two Series. In Stephenson's best offensive season, 1929, as I indicated earlier, each of the three Cubs starting outfielders (Stephenson, Cuyler, and Wilson) had over 100 RBIs, the only time such a feat has been accomplished in National League history.

At .336, Riggs Stephenson's lifetime batting average is the highest of any eligible batter who is not in the Hall of Fame, ranks 22nd all-time in Major League Baseball, and still leads all players in the history of the Chicago National League Ball Club.[43] Admittedly, his batting numbers were inflated somewhat by playing during the live-ball era, and he never led the league in batting average (or, indeed, in any offensive category except doubles in 1927). Still, he was a patient hitter, walking exactly twice as often as he struck out (494 to 247), and he had some power, leading to a lifetime .880 OPS (.868 with the Cubs).

Although there is some truth to the standard "what might have been" narrative, Stephenson's career was far from a failure. Had he played 50 years later, when his shoulder could have been surgically repaired and he consequently could have had much more playing time, Stephenson would certainly be in the Hall of Fame. Were it not for the incomparable Billy Williams, Riggs Stephenson would probably be remembered as the greatest Cubs left fielder of all time.

Riggs played for a few years in the minor leagues after his major league career ended abruptly in 1934 due to the accumulated injuries, finally retiring in 1939. Stephenson returned to his home state of Alabama, where he was inducted into the state Sports Hall of Fame in 1971. He ran a car dealership in Tuscaloosa and a lumber yard for many years, and passed away on November 15, 1985 at the age of 87. Obviously, his shoulder problems had no effect on his longevity.

## Hazen (Kiki) Cuyler

---

[43] www.baseball-reference.com

Hazen Shirley – don't call me Shirley![44] - Cuyler was born on August 31, 1898 in Harrisville, Michigan. After briefly attending the U.S. Military Academy at West Point, Cuyler returned to Michigan, married his high school sweetheart, and worked, as so many people did in that part of the country in those days, in the auto industry for General Motors. Playing for a company baseball team, his talent was noticed and he actually changed positions in the company, moving from Flint to Detroit, so he could play in a "faster" league, from which he was signed by the Pittsburgh Pirates in 1920.

Cuyler spent most of the next three years in the minors, finally cracking the Pirate starting lineup in 1924, when he hit an impressive .354/.402/.539. The following year, he did even better, .357/.423/.598, scoring 144 runs in 153 games, and leading the Pirates to the 1925 NL title and World Series championship; he drove in the Series-winning run with a two-out, two-run double off the great Walter Johnson in the eighth inning of game seven. During that 1925 season, he had a career-high 18 homers, including two inside-the-park home runs on August 28 at the tiny Baker Bowl in Philadelphia. In all, Cuyler hit eight inside-the-park homers in 1925. It took until 1979 -- when Willie Wilson had five -- for someone to have even close to that many in a season. He'd have won the MVP award easily (he finished second in the voting), except that Rogers Hornsby that year happened to hit .403 with 39 home runs and 143 RBI, winning the Triple Crown and the MVP. Still, the voting was close -- Hornsby had 73 points and Cuyler finished second with 61.

From there, though, things went completely downhill with the Pirates for Cuyler. Kiki and the Pirates had a contract dispute before the 1927 season, and then-new Pirate manager Donie Bush asked him to play center field and bat second; Cuyler felt himself more effective hitting third. The feud came to a head when Cuyler didn't slide into second base to break up a double play late in the year. Bush benched him for the rest of the season and for the entire World Series as well -- something that clearly didn't help the ballclub, although it isn't likely that any team would have defeated one of the greatest teams of all

---

[44] Leslie Nielsen's line from *Airplane*

time, the 1927 Yankees. (That's the year Babe Ruth hit 60 home runs and Lou Gehrig hit 47.)

Knowing that Cuyler was on the outs with the Bucs, the Cubs got him for virtually nothing on November 28, 1927, sending a journeyman infielder (Sparky Adams) and outfielder (Pete Scott) for a 28-year-old career .300 hitter who had already been in the top 10 of MVP voting results twice.

Returned to his normal batting and fielding slots as a Cub, Cuyler had a decent .285/.359/.473 year in 1928, and then exploded in 1929, the pennant year; he hit .360/.438/.532 and led the National League with 43 stolen bases (one of four times he led the NL in steals), as the Cubs won the pennant for the first time in a decade. The stolen base number is even more impressive given that steals were becoming less important in an era given over to power hitters. The next NL player to steal more than Cuyler's 43 in 1929 was Maury Wills, with 50 in 1960.

Cuyler's best overall year with the Cubs was probably the 1929 season, but an argument can also be made for his 1930 campaign, where he scored an eye-popping 155 runs (good for 24th on the all time single season list), batting often in front of Hack Wilson as Hack drove in a record 191 runs. Cuyler drove in 134 himself, ranking a distant second on the club. Naturally, all 1930 stats have to be looked at with a somewhat skeptical eye due to the "juiced" nature of the ball that year, but those figures are impressive nonetheless. During that 1930 season, Kiki hit an extra-inning walkoff home run in the most attended single game in Wrigley Field history, the June 27 Ladies Day game, seen by 51,556.[45] In those days, there were more seats to begin with, and they used to cram people in the aisles; this practice went on until the 1970's, when the Fire Department put an end to it. To this day, you can see the fire code signs around various areas of the ballpark, stating the maximum safe capacity of each area.

---

[45] Ladies Day n baseball was started by Chicago Cub executive Margaret Donahue, one of the first female executives in baseball.

Kiki suffered a broken foot during the 1932 season, causing him to miss a third of the year. When he returned, he put the entire ballclub on his back and almost singlehandedly carried the Cubs to the pennant. He hit .365 from August 27 to the end of the season. Moreover, he hit a walkoff homer in one of the most dramatic games in team history on August 31. Bill Veeck said it was the best game he ever saw in person. For a while it held the reputation of being perhaps the greatest single Cubs moment, until Gabby Hartnett's "Homer in the Gloamin" came along six years later, and Cuyler's game is now forgotten except by baseball history buffs. The Cubs, as usual, failed to win the World Series in 1932.

Cuyler broke his leg during spring training in 1933, which caused him to miss half of the season, and his production began to decline. In 1935, slowing down at age 36, he was released in mid-season and picked up by Cincinnati, finishing his career with the Brooklyn Dodgers in 1938. He finished with 2299 hits; if not for the injuries, perhaps the Cubs would have kept him and he might have approached a 3000-hit career.

Off the field, Cuyler was regarded as a gentleman during a time where many players were thought of as rather loud, crude, and drank too much – see Hack Wilson. He became an idol to women, and as a devoutly religious man, he prayed and crossed himself during games, perhaps the first player to do this in public. (Tony Taylor of the Cubs was the first player that I personally ever saw perform this ritual.) His nickname of "Kiki" is derived from the sound of the first part of his last name, so it is pronounced "Cuy-Cuy" and not "Kee-Kee."

After retiring as a player, Cuyler stayed in baseball, managing in the minor leagues (winning the Southern Association pennant in his first year managing, in 1939 at Chattanooga), and then returning to the major leagues as a Cubs coach. He eventually wound up as a coach for the Boston Red Sox, and he was working for them when he suffered a fatal heart attack shortly before he was to depart for spring training in 1950, dying on February 11, 1950 in Ann Arbor, Michigan, at only 51. He is buried in his hometown of Harrisville, Michigan, a small town about 150 miles north of where he began his journey into baseball in Flint.

Cuyler was given baseball's highest honor posthumously in 1968 when the Veterans Committee made him a Hall of Famer. One of the greatest Cub players of all time was certainly deserving of the recognition.

## Hack Wilson

Short but barrel-chested Lewis Robert Hack Wilson was the centerfielder in this group. Wilson is best remembered today for his single-season record of 191 runs batted in, a record that has never been surpassed in almost 90 years of baseball since then. But his drinking kept him from being an even greater player and having an even longer career. As one writer put it, "Hack Wilson usually played in the outfield, but I'd put him at first base if I was the manager because he wouldn't have as far to stagger to the dugout."[46]

Hack Wilson's career somewhat mirrored that of the United States of the 1920's and 30's. His carefree, live for today attitude – a hallmark of the Roaring 20's - may have served him well in the 20's, but led to a fairly early exit from baseball in the 30's. Hack stood only 5'6" but weighed at least 190 pounds. He had massive shoulders, a barrel

---

[46] Mike Royko, *Chicago Sun Times*, 1981

chest, a protruding stomach, and his neck measured 18 inches around. His short arms and short legs were very thick, but he had small feet – size six. By contrast, I am 5'10" and 175 pounds and have size 10 shoes, which is fairly normal.

Wilson was a surprisingly able outfielder, even though one of the most famous incidents of his career centered on fielding misadventures. In the 1929 World Series, he somehow lost two fly balls in the sun during the same inning, helping the Philadelphia Athletics to score 10 runs against the Cubs and erase an 8-0 Cub lead. (Remember, after all, this is the Cubs.)

Wilson was born in Ellwood City, Pennsylvania, in 1900. He quit school in the sixth grade and worked as a printer's apprentice, an ironworker in a locomotive factory and a shipyard laborer, among other jobs. He eventually made his way into baseball, joining Martinsburg of the Blue Ridge League as a catcher in 1921. In 1922, he hit 30 home runs in 84 games to win a promotion to Portsmouth of the Virginia League, where he was switched to the outfield.

When Wilson led the league in triples, home runs, RBI, and batting average, the New York Giants brought him up to the majors. New York's clubhouse man despaired of finding a uniform to fit his odd dimensions. Finally, manager John McGraw tossed the outfielder one from his own locker. "Don't disgrace that uniform," he growled. "A great player once wore it. Me!" "A great player will wear it now," said Wilson modestly.

He acquired the nickname "Hack" while he was with the Giants, because of his resemblance to the famous wrestler and strongman George Hackenschmidt, the "Russian Lion."

Others insisted he was named after Hack Miller, a Cubs outfielder reputed to be the strongest man in baseball. Still others noted his resemblance to a taxicab, and a few thought the name came from the way Wilson had played the outfield before he had mastered the niceties of his position.

**George Hackenschmidt, the "Russian Lion", circa 1910**

**If you think about it long enough, Hack Wilson does kind of look like a taxicab.**

Wilson was a decent enough player with the Giants, but his off-field antics and happy-go-lucky attitude annoyed McGraw, who took a much more serious approach to the game of baseball than Hack did.

When Wilson started slowly in 1925, New York optioned him to Toledo. Then, through what McGraw always insisted was a clerical error, the Giants failed to renew their option on Wilson and he was drafted by the Cubs. (Yet another great move by the Cubs!)

The big-shouldered Wilson instantly took to the City of the Big Shoulders. In 1926, he led the National League with 21 homers while batting .321 with 109 RBIs. The next year, he tied Philadelphia's Cy Williams for the homer lead with 30 and upped his RBI total to 129. In 1928, he and St. Louis' Jim Bottomley shared the home run crown with 31 each.

A large part of Wilson's success was due to the careful handling of Cubs manager Joe McCarthy. The Cubs skipper knew when to pat him on the back and when to bawl him out. He could not prevent Wilson from drinking – no one could - but did manage to slow him down. He also protected Wilson from the wrath of owner Philip K. Wrigley, a strong prohibitionist.

Wilson's numbers improved each season. In 1929, his 39 home runs just missed leading the league, but he did manage to top the N.L. in RBI with 159. He also batted .345 and helped the Cubs win their first pennant since 1918. He was criticized after losing the two fly balls in the sun during the Cubs' World Series loss to the Athletics.

But McCarthy had completely rebuilt the slugger's ego by the 1930 season, and Wilson had one of the most remarkable offensive seasons on record. He hit .356, set the N.L. record for home runs with 56 – which lasted until the steroid era - and knocked in 191 base runners for a major-league record. As with Joe DiMaggio's 56-game hitting streak, Wilson's RBI record appears likely to last forever. He also established National League records for extra-base hits (97) and total bases (423) in one season, and set the Cubs' single-season marks for slugging percentage (.723), RBI in a month (53), and home runs both at home (33) and on the road (23) with that incredible season. NOTE: I don't think the entire team had 53 RBI's in any month in 2012, 2013, or 2014.

McCarthy left the Cubs to manage the Yankees after the 1930 season. His replacement was the blunt and brusque Rogers Hornsby, who had none of McCarthy's interpersonal skills. Under Hornsby's unrelenting criticism, Wilson struggled. In 1931, he hit only 13 homers with 61 RBI and a .261 batting average.

After 1931, the Cubs dealt him to the Cardinals, who passed him on to Brooklyn before he had played an inning. He had a fair season with the Dodgers in 1932 but then hit the skids for good. By 1935, he was back in the minor leagues, trying unsuccessfully to make a comeback in Albany. And probably drinking too much all along the way.

Wilson died in 1948 at the age of 48. Wilson's 12-year major-league record shows a .307 batting average, 244 home runs and 1,062 RBI. Many players have better totals, but few have come close to matching his best seasons. After a long campaign, his admirers finally convinced the Veterans Committee to name Wilson to the Hall of Fame in 1979.

Wilson's .590 career slugging percentage is tops for the Cubs in the 1900s. His .322 career batting average as a Cub ranks seventh in club history, and Wilson also can be found among the team's top 10 in home runs (ninth, 190).

# 15 CHARLIE ROOT

If we were to ask the name of the Cubs' all-time winningest pitcher – wins as a member of the Chicago Cubs, that is – most people would probably say Ferguson Jenkins. A few really astute people would say Mordecai Brown, and many younger fans would say something like Kerry Wood or Greg Maddux. The answer is none of those, but a fellow who pitched in the 1920's and 1930's for the Cubs, named Charles Henry Root.

In fact, in 1985, SABR (The Society for American Baseball Research) – baseball's version of computer geeks - held its national convention in Chicago. One of the most anticipated events at all such gatherings is the trivia contest, featuring renowned experts in all aspects of the game and its history. Seldom does a question stump all the contestants. The moderator of the panel, injecting some local flavor into the queries, asked: "Who holds the Cubs record for most career pitching wins?" No one at the table knew.[47]

**Charlie Root**

---

[47] www.bleedcubbieblue.com

In his long Cubs career, Root set team records for wins (201 – 100 percent of his wins in the major leagues), games (605), innings (3137.1), and seasons (16). He ranks second in complete games, strikeouts, and walks. Root pitched for the Cubs between 1926 and 1941; between 1926 and 1933, his win totals were 18, 26, 14, 19, 16, 17, 15, and 15.

Charles Henry Root was born March 17, 1899, in Middletown, Ohio – so called because it is about halfway between Dayton and Cincinnati. Root quit school when he was only 13 years old and began working by driving a grocery wagon while spending most of his free time playing baseball. While pitching for the town team, he was seen and signed by the St. Louis Browns, for whom he made his major league debut in 1923. He finished 0-4, his only non-Cub big league decisions. After two years in the minors in Los Angeles, Root came to the majors to stay, with the Cubs, in 1926.

Root was a right-handed pitcher and batter, the only things he did right-handed in his life. He immediately became the workhorse of the staff, 18-17 in his rookie year. In 1927, he had his best year, 26-15 (his only 20-game season, and the last Cub to win 25). In 1929, the Cubs won the first of their four pennants during Root's tenure. Charlie's record that season was 19-6, and manager Joe McCarthy assigned him the opening game of the World Series, at Wrigley Field.

It was the first of an astonishing trio of World Series games in which Root would be on the losing side of an historic performance. Surprise starter Howard Ehmke won the game for the Philadelphia Athletics, striking out a record thirteen batters.

Root started game five in Philadelphia, and carried an 8-0 lead into the seventh inning. But the Athletics then scored ten runs, most ever in a Series inning, aided by two fly balls lost by Hack Wilson in the centerfield sun. One of the lost flies went for a three-run, inside-the-park homer.

Root was 15-10 during the Cubs' next pennant-winning year, 1932. The Cubs lost the first two games of the World Series to the Yankees in New York, and Root started game three, October 1, at Wrigley. (more later on that.)

Charlie lasted in the majors into his early forties, a veteran of four great managerial regimes: McCarthy, Hornsby, Hartnett, and Grimm. Late in the 1941 season, he announced his major league retirement effective the end of the year. August 10 was "Charlie Root Day" at Wrigley Field, and Root lost the game to the Reds and Johnny Vander Meer, 3-1.

Root's 200th win came in Boston, in relief, on August 27, 1941, and he provided the winning margin with a bases-loaded single in the ninth inning. Root then began a long minor league pitching career, pitching until the age of 49. In 1942, for example, he joined the Hollywood Stars of the Pacific Coast League, and he was player-manager of the club in 1943 and 1944. He followed that with a two-year stint as player-manager of the Columbus Red Birds. Charlie ended his playing career in 1948, while serving as skipper of the Billings Mustangs. Root won 111 minor league games, for a combined 312 professional wins over 27 seasons. Root managed in the minors after hanging up his glove for good, and returned to the Cubs as pitching coach, serving from 1951-53. He coached for the Milwaukee Braves in 1956 and 1957, and had a final coaching stint with the Cubs in 1960. I guess you could call him a baseball "lifer."

Root also owned a cattle ranch and an antique shop in Hollister, California, not far from the movie studios. He was invited to attend the filming of "The Babe Ruth Story" (William Bendix in the title role), and accepted. He must have sensed what was coming, but refused an offer to portray himself on screen in the called shot scene; saying he would not be party to a falsehood.

In 1969, Major League Baseball sponsored a number of elections, to celebrate the supposed 100th anniversary of professional ball. Participants were journalists and scholars, voting on the greatest players of all-time, and of individual teams. Root was elected the greatest Cubs right-handed pitcher. More recently, Fergie Jenkins, by sheer weight of his multiple 20-game seasons and eventual Hall of Fame career, is usually accorded that title.

Root died in Hollister on November 5, 1970 at the age of 71.

**Warming up for one of his 201 wins, no doubt**

## The Called Shot

Babe Ruth's famous "called shot" game from the 1932 World Series between the Yankees and the Cubs is all about the myth of whether or not Ruth did point at center field while at bat in the fifth inning, after making some sort of gesture just before that at Cubs pitcher Charlie Root after Root got two strikes on the Babe.

It was rowdy from the start of the game, as the Yankees scored three times before the first out of the game, capped by a three-run homer from Babe Ruth. Ruth nearly duplicated the home run in the second inning, hitting a deep drive that was caught by Kiki Cuyler at the right field wall. Gehrig homered to lead off the third inning. But the Cubs came back to tie the game, 4-4. The tying run reached base in the fourth inning when Ruth awkwardly misplayed a Bill Jurges fly ball into a double. In the Yankee fifth, Joe Sewell led off with a groundout, bringing Ruth to the plate for the third time that afternoon. Then, as the legend goes, Ruth, two strikes down, pointed to center field in response to the taunting of Cub players, and delivered the next pitch to the very spot he had indicated.

Newsreel footage exists of the home run, and of some of the pitches Ruth took (the home run was the only swing in the at-bat), but not of the banter between pitches, as the cameras were shut off during down time. In recent years, two home movies of the sequence came to light, both portraying several gestures by Ruth. They are taken from distinctly different angles; the more publicized of the two is ambiguous, with most observers seeing the direction of the gestures as toward the Cubs dugout. The other film is less ambiguous, and seems to confirm the direction as the dugout.

Similarly the eyewitness recollections of players and fans are so varied and contradictory that a researcher is forced to consider the sum of it worthless. Cub public address announcer Pat Pieper[48] and retired Associate Supreme Court Justice John Paul Stevens – a Chicagoan and Cub fan – believe Ruth definitely called the shot, while others, including players on the field like Yankee catcher Bill Dickey – state that Ruth was just mad and was pointing at the Cub pitcher or even the Cub dugout.

For his part, when it became apparent that the incident would haunt him all his life, Root bore it as best he could. He could be belligerent ("I'd have knocked him on his ass"), or almost plaintive ("Please, he didn't point"). This was a blow to a great athlete's professional pride, and Root never fully lived it down. But it would have made for a great Abbott and Costello routine – Root pitching to Ruth!

---

[48] Pat Pieper was the Chicago Cub field announcer from 1916 to 1974 – some 59 years. I remember him very well. He had a distinctive way of announcing the starting lineups for the game – "Have your pencils and scorecards ready, and I'll give you the correct lineups for today's game" was the way he introduced the lineups for every game that I can remember. Remember, the last 20+ years of his games were also on WGN television.

**Did Babe Ruth actually call his home run shot?**

# 16 GABBY HARTNETT

Great Chicago Cub catchers are few and far between, but there have been a few of them.

The greatest Cub catcher of all time was easily Charles Leo (Gabby) Hartnett – sorry Randy Hundley and Jody Davis fans as well as those who remember Johnny Kling from the early 1900's – but this one is not even close. Nicknamed Gabby because of his soft-spoken nature and never one to waste words, Gabby Hartnett is still probably the best catcher in the history of the National League, although Johnny Bench is right up there also.

In his 20-year career, from 1922 to 1941, in which all but 54 games were with the Cubs, Gabby had a lifetime average of .297, on-base percentage of .370, 1912 hits, and 236 home runs. Pretty good stats, especially for a catcher.

Charles Leo Hartnett was born on December 20, 1900, in Woonsocket, Rhode Island, the eldest of 14 children born to Fred and Ellen "Nell" Hartnett. Fred, a laborer, moved his family to Millville, Massachusetts, just over the state line from Woonsocket, when he took a job at Banigan's Millville Rubber Shop. Fred played semipro baseball in his younger years and managed the Millville town team for a period, and was considered to have a tremendous throwing arm. It was a legacy he passed to his son, Leo.

Charles, known as Leo, grew up listening to his father talk baseball. As soon as Leo was able, he began playing baseball, and gravitated to the role of catcher, just as his father had. At 14 Leo finished the eighth grade at Longfellow Grammar School and took a job as a laborer at the Rubber Shop[49]. He also joined the town's baseball team, along with another future professional, Tim McNamara, who went to Fordham University and pitched for the Boston Braves and New York Giants from 1922 through 1926. (Lifetime record of 14-29 and an ERA of almost five.) Though Leo later left the Rubber Shop to attend the prestigious Dean Academy in nearby Franklin, Massachusetts, it was on the baseball diamond that he got his real education.

Charles Leo had a terrific throwing arm, so good that in 1920 the American Steel and Wire Company in Worcester offered him a job in its shipping department just so he could play on the company baseball team. (Don't think this kind of recruiting only happens in sports. The great singer/movie star Howard Keel – *Kiss Me Kate, Seven Brides for Seven Brothers, Kismet, Annie Get Your Gun* – worked at a McDonnell-Douglas plant during WWII but also was part of that employer's touring company that put on shows for local audiences in the Los Angeles area. That is how Keel got discovered.)

Hartnett thrived, perhaps even discovering that work was occasionally getting in the way of baseball, instead of the reverse. There is a story, impossible to prove but widely recounted and intriguing, that the New York Giants' John McGraw heard of Hartnett and sent scout Jesse Burkett to have a look at the prospect. Evidently Burkett felt the catcher's hands were too small for major-league baseball, so the Giants passed. What is a matter of record is

---

[49] An awfully high percentage of people in those days – including my grandparents - never went to school past the eighth grade. High school graduation was not that common then.

that Hartnett signed his first professional baseball contract with the Worcester Boosters of the Class A Eastern League on March 12, 1921.

Appearing in 100 games for Worcester, Hartnett played well enough that Cubs scout Jack Doyle offered him $2,500 to sign with Chicago. Leo accepted and the Cubs sent him to spring training with the team on Catalina Island, off the Southern California coast. Hartnett did not immediately impress manager Bill Killefer, who already had Bob O'Farrell on the roster as his primary backstop, and it took Doyle's intervention to persuade Killefer to give Hartnett a legitimate trial at catcher. The manager had the youngster catch Grover Cleveland Alexander for a full game, and afterward the pitcher told his manager that Hartnett was "all right." That verdict was enough to keep Leo on the Chicago roster.

Backing up starting catcher O'Farrell in 1922, the 21-year-old Hartnett barely spoke to anyone, especially not to newspaper reporters. In view of his awkward shyness, teammates and the press dubbed him Gabby, an ironic moniker at the time, but one that he actually grew into as he aged, developing a reputation as something of a chatterbox crouched behind home plate.

After making his major-league debut on April 12, 1922, at age 21, Hartnett appeared in only 34 games and collected a mere 14 hits for the season. Behind the plate, though, he made only two errors, a mark that highlighted his value as a defensive backup and kept him on the roster for the next season. In 1923 Gabby's batting average climbed over 70 points, and when O'Farrell was injured in 1924, Hartnett was ready. Making the most of the opportunity, he hit .299 and homered 16 times in 111 games, and finished tied for 15th in voting for the National League's Most Valuable Player. (The Cub version of the Lou Gehrig story, with Gehrig taking over at first base from Wally Pipp, and that was it for Pipp as a Yankee first baseman.)

From then on Hartnett played his position better than any of his predecessors and most of his successors. Large for the time, the 6-foot-1, 195-pound Gabby became the first player to hit five or more homers in the first six games of a season, and then went on to break the single-season record for home runs by a catcher in 1925 with 24. In spite of a late-season slump, he finished second in the league in home runs, trailing only Rogers Hornsby's 39. In 1924 and 1925, only 136 bases were swiped off Hartnett, compared with a league average of 178 against other starting catchers. During his 1926 season he threw out 60 percent of the runners attempting steals against him while finishing third among National League catchers in assists and tied for third in putouts. So for all of you who want to place Mike Piazza ahead of Hartnett, consider that Piazza was nowhere near the defensive catcher that Hartnett was. Not even close.

Hartnett's 1927 season saw his offensive production increase to the point that he finished tenth in the league's Most Valuable Player balloting. The Cubs carried two catchers for most of the year, 26-year-old Gabby and Cuban-born Mike Gonzalez, a decade older. Hartnett carried the brunt of the catching load for the fourth-place team, appearing in 127 games while improving his batting average to .294, and leading the league in putouts, assists, errors, and runners caught stealing.

Gabby continued to improve the following year, 1928, with a .302 batting average, 26 doubles, 9 triples, and 14 homers in only 388 at-bats, but the Cubs managed only a one-place improvement, to third. He also earned yet another nickname. "As he grew older and added weight, the big catcher developed a ruddy complexion, resulting in the nickname 'Old Tomato Face,'" a biographer wrote.

As spring training began in 1929, on Catalina Island[50] just off the coast of Los Angeles, Hartnett and his new bride, Martha Henrietta (Marshall) Hartnett, planned to use the trip as both preseason conditioning and a honeymoon on the isolated resort. The couple, married on January 28, had a son, Charles Leo Jr. (known as Bud, not Gabby Junior), born in December 1931, and a daughter, Sheila, born

---

[50] The Cubs trained on Catalina Island in California every spring from 1921-1941, and from 1946-51. (The island was controlled by the U.S. military during the war years. Eventually the Cubs moved to Arizona for spring training.)

in June 1935.[51]

Because of unexplained deadness in his throwing arm, Gabby only made 22 plate appearances in 1929. Unable to throw well and unresponsive to treatment, Hartnett basically rested for the year. While he did come to bat three times as a pinch-hitter during the 1929 World Series against the Philadelphia Athletics, he did not record a hit.

Whatever the cause of the malady, Hartnett recovered to the point that he was able to post a .339 batting average in 1930, with career highs in hits (172), runs scored (84), home runs (37), RBIs (122), slugging (.630) and OPS (1.034), while committing only eight errors in 136 games behind the plate. Also, on the defensive side, Hartnett led the league catchers in putouts (646), assists (68), and runners caught stealing (36).[52]

It was about this time that Gabby got into trouble with the Commissioner of Baseball, his one such reprimand, and it could only have happened in Chicago. Al Capone, by the late 1920's/early `30s, felt secure enough in his "position" as head of the Chicago mob to try to acquire some respectability. One reasonable way to do this was to appear in public at popular sporting events, like any legitimate celebrity; and he and his considerable entourage became regulars at Wrigley Field. Even after Al's imprisonment, the Capone gang continued to attend. Bill Veeck Jr once said: "Whenever I saw a $100 bill (in the box office till) I knew Ralph Capone (Al's brother) and his boys were at the game."

---

[51] Ronald Reagan got his start in show business by covering Chicago Cubs games. On a 1937 trip to California to cover baseball spring training for the Cubs, Reagan took a screen test for Warner Brothers' film studios and was signed to a contract. If not for the Cubs, Ronald Reagan may never have been President of the United States.

[52] Again, remember that catchers' mitts were nowhere near the quality they are today, and errors were therefore more frequent.

But there's more to this story. Hartnett once obligingly signed a ball for Capone and a young friend at Capone's request, the moment immortalized by a newspaper photographer. When the photo circulated, an edict came down from Commissioner Landis' office forbidding fraternization between players and fans. Hartnett's reply to Landis' admonishments became legendary: "If you don't want anybody to talk to the Big Guy, Judge, *you* tell him."

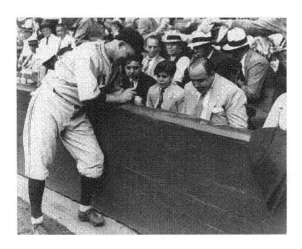

**Gabby Hartnett signing an autograph at Wrigley Field for none other than Al Capone.**

As it turns out, Al Capone was a huge baseball fan and a huge Cub fan. He went to Cub games virtually every day of the season. In the late 1920's, he actually wanted to buy the Cubs, but of course, Major League Baseball would never have approved that sale. But one interesting note: He said the first thing he would do if he owned the Cubs was bring in black players – he thought baseball was missing a huge marketing opportunity by failing to have African American players on the team. If Capone would have been able to purchase the Cubs, baseball would have been integrated around 1927 instead of 20 years later in 1947. [53]

In 1932 the Cubs won the pennant by four games over the Pittsburgh

---

[53] From *Get Capone*, by Jonathan Eig, published in 2010

Pirates, and faced the Yankees in the World Series. The Cubs' pitchers sported the lowest earned-run average in the league that year (3.44), in part due to Hartnett's experience calling the games. During the top of the fifth inning in game three of the Series, Hartnett was behind the plate when Babe Ruth allegedly – see Charlie Root - raised his arm and gestured toward the pitcher and the outfield. According to Hartnett biographer William McNeil, Gabby later said, "I don't want to take anything from the Babe, because he's the reason we made good money, but he didn't call the shot. He held up the index finger of his left hand ... and said, 'It only takes one to hit.'" Regardless of whether Ruth did or did not "call his shot," the story refuses to fade with time.

Hartnett, however, certainly did not let the Series loss affect him. At the top of his game, he was selected as a National League reserve in the inaugural All-Star Game. The next year, batting .336 with 13 home runs by the time of the game, he was named the starting catcher in a battery with Giants ace Carl Hubbell. It was in the top of the first inning, after a leadoff single by Charlie Gehringer and a walk to Heinie Manush, that Hubbell started his historic streak. He struck out Ruth, Lou Gehrig, and Jimmie Foxx to end the inning, and then picked up where he left off in the second, whiffing Al Simmons and Joe Cronin before Bill Dickey broke up the string with a base hit. Hartnett went 0-for-2 at the plate, but never played a more memorable All Star Game.

The following season, 1935, was one of Hartnett's best. His body was 34 years old, but he played as if he were ten years younger. He batted .344, made only nine errors in 110 games and led the Cubs to the World Series against the Detroit Tigers. Hartnett played well that postseason, batting .292, but the Cubs fell in six games in the Series. After the season he was named the National League's Most Valuable Player, over pitcher Dizzy Dean of the St. Louis Cardinals and Arky Vaughn of the Pittsburgh Pirates, a small comfort for again falling short of a championship.

In 1937 Harnett was again selected for the All Star Game, his fifth consecutive appearance, and was behind the plate paired with Cardinal rival pitcher Dizzy Dean. In the bottom of the third inning, with two outs and the game scoreless, Dean gave up a single to Joe DiMaggio and a home run to Lou Gehrig. Earl Averill then hit a sharp drive directly back to the mound, a hit so hard that it clipped the pitcher's left foot before finding second baseman Billy Herman's glove for the eventual throw and the putout at first base. Dean left the game, his career changed forever. Averill's low line shot had broken the big toe on Dean's left foot, and when Dizzy tried to come back before it had fully healed, he altered his delivery to avoid the pain. That caused Dean to permanently damage his arm and finally retire from the game prematurely (but not before pitching for three seasons for the Hartnett-managed Cubs).[54]

Hartnett finished a close second behind the Cardinals' Joe Medwick in MVP voting in 1937, but he saved his greatest moment for 1938, and another Chicago pennant race. On July 20, 1938, the Cubs languished in third place in the standings, 5½ games behind league leader Pittsburgh, despite having won seven straight games after a six-game losing skid during the preceding two weeks. Chicago owner Philip Wrigley fired established manager Charlie Grimm and replaced him with catcher Hartnett. The move worked. By late September the Cubs were 1½ games out of first and had a three-game series in Chicago remaining with the Pirates. After the Cubs won the first game to pull within a half-game of the lead, the teams met again at Wrigley Field on September 28. That was the date of Gabby's famous "Homer in the Gloamin" that propelled the Cubs to the 1938 pennant. The Cubs won the pennant but once again lost the World Series.

Hartnett, now under media scrutiny as the Cubs' manager, began to show the strain in 1939. He was accused by some players of favoring pitcher Dizzy Dean; there were other petty squabbles; and Gabby found himself catching more often than he'd have liked simply because his was the best bat on the team among the catchers. On August 28, 1939, Hartnett's durability was formally acknowledged when he caught his 1,728th game, breaking Ray Schalk's major-league

---

[54] Dizzy Dean was 27 at the time. He won 134 games through 1937 but only 16 after that. He did have a great career as a radio announcer after that, however.

record for games caught by a catcher. (The record has since been broken by several catchers and Hartnett is now in 13th place.)

After the 1940 season, following nearly two decades with the club and despite a three-season record of 203-176 (.536), Hartnett was abruptly fired as manager on November 13. Less than a month later, on December 10, he signed as a player-coach with the New York Giants, and, at the age of 40, hit .300 in 64 games in 1941. On September 24 of that season, Hartnett went 1-for-4 against the Philadelphia Phillies in what proved to be his final big-league game.

Not quite done with baseball, Hartnett managed five seasons in the minors from 1942 through 1946. In 1942 he managed Indianapolis of the American Association to a 76-78 record, and from 1943 through 1945 managed Jersey City of the International League. In 1946, his final year managing, he managed Buffalo of the International League.

After retiring from baseball, Hartnett opened Gabby Hartnett's Recreation Center in Lincolnwood, a Chicago suburb. The enterprise ultimately grew to 20 bowling lanes, a barbershop, a soda fountain, a cocktail lounge, and a sporting-goods store. On January 26, 1955, with a career major-league batting average of .297, 1,912 hits, and one of the most famous home runs in the history of the game, he was elected to the Baseball Hall of Fame with an illustrious class that also included Joe DiMaggio, Ted Lyons, and Dazzy Vance.

Hartnett lived his entire post-baseball life in Illinois. He was a coach and scout for the Kansas City Athletics for two years in the mid-1960s, but spent much of his time playing golf, hunting, and enjoying his golden years. Eventually his health deteriorated. In 1969 he was taken to the hospital after spitting blood on the golf course. The next year his spleen was removed, but it was an unwinnable fight. At 5:20 A.M. on his 72nd birthday, December 20, 1972, in Park Ridge, Illinois, Gabby Hartnett died of complications from cirrhosis of the liver.[55] He is buried in All Saints Cemetery in Des Plaines, Illinois. Gabby is a near-neighbor of Harry Caray, who is also buried at All

---

[55] Park Ridge, Illinois is my hometown and also the hometown of my even more famous classmate, Hillary Clinton.

Saints.

## Hartnett's "Homer in the Gloamin'"

September 28, 1938 was a gray, gloomy afternoon at Wrigley Field, with 34,465 fans assembled for the crucial game between the Cubs and the Pittsburgh Pirates. Game time, in those days, was 3 p.m., thus it was well past 5 p.m. when the ninth inning began, with the score tied, 5-5.

By all accounts, plate umpire George Barr announced, after the conclusion of the eighth inning, that play would halt after the ninth, if the score remained even. This was not uncommon. The game would have ended in a tie, and necessitated a doubleheader the following day. Both teams were duly informed, and Cubs pitcher Charlie Root set the Pirates down in order in the top of the ninth. Pittsburgh reliever Mace Brown retired the first two Cubs, Cavarretta and Reynolds, bringing Hartnett to the plate. Brown used the reduced visibility to his advantage and got two quick fastball strikes on the catcher. With darkness setting in and visibility decreasing, Brown inexplicably threw Hartnett a high curve. Gabby knocked the pitch over the fence in left-center field, and into immortality. According to one reporter, most fans were unable to follow the flight of the ball in the darkness, but when it settled into the left field seats for a walk-off home run, Wrigley Field erupted with a deafening roar that could be heard for blocks. Thousands of … spectators came spilling out of the stands screaming and racing toward the diamond.

Hartnett later said, "I swung with everything I had, and then I got that feeling, the kind of feeling you get when the blood rushes out of your head and you get dizzy. A lot of people have told me they didn't know the ball was in the bleachers. Well, I did. Maybe I was the only one in the park who did. I knew the moment I hit it. … I don't think I saw third base … and I don't think I walked a step to the plate – I was carried in." The "Homer in the Gloamin'," as it is remembered, remains one of the signature walk-off home runs of all time. The Cubs won again the next day to complete a series sweep of the Pirates. The 10-1 victory capped a ten-game Chicago winning streak that placed the Cubs on the path to win the NL pennant by two games. The ending was not entirely happy, however, as the Cubs were swept in the World Series by the Yankees. Where have we heard that before?

Nevertheless, Charles Leo Hartnett remains the greatest catcher in the history of the Chicago Cubs and one of the two greatest catchers in the history of the National League.

# 17 BILLY HERMAN

Billy Herman – not to be confused with Babe Herman, another stellar player who actually played for the Cubs in 1933-1935 - was the second baseman on those great Cub teams that won pennants in 1932, 1935, and 1938. He teamed with Stan Hack at third base, Woody English and then Billy Jurges at shortstop, and Charlie Grimm and then Rip Collins at first base.

"Baseball was always kind of a struggle for me," Billy Herman once said. "I guess maybe I was doing all right and didn't realize it, but it always seemed like a struggle to me." Apparently it was not THAT much of a struggle, since he posted a lifetime average of .304, had 2,345 total hits, finished in the top ten in the league in hits ten times and first once, and was voted into the Hall of Fame by the Veterans' Committee in 1975. He was also a ten-time All Star.

William Jennings Bryan Herman – named for the famed politician[56] - was born in New Albany, Indiana, right across the Ohio River from Louisville, Kentucky, on July 7, 1909. As we have seen in some other top 100 profiles of players born in that era, he was named after a popular politician of his day. During his playing career he was known for his stellar defense and consistent batting; in fact, he still holds many National League defensive records for second basemen.

He attended New Albany High School, and began playing in the minor leagues in 1927, right out of high school. He broke into the majors in 1931 at age 21 when the Chicago Cubs purchased his contract from Louisville for $50,000. Billy asserted himself as a star the following season, starting all 154 games in 1932 and had 206 hits, scored 102 runs and had a .314 batting average. He also helped the Chicago Cubs to the World Series. He finished ninth in MVP balloting. Though Herman missed the inaugural All-Star Game in 1933, he was named to the next 10 in a row.

A fixture in the Chicago lineup over the next decade, Herman was a consistent hitter and solid run producer. He regularly hit .300 or higher (high of .341 in 1935) and drove in a high of 93 runs in 1936.

Herman's best season came in 1935 when he helped lead the Cubs to the National League pennant. He led baseball with 227 hits and 57 doubles and hit a career-high .341. 1935 was one of three seasons when Herman had more than 200 hits, and it earned him a fourth place finish in the MVP voting, which was won by his teammate Gabby Hartnett.

The next four seasons were a string of good to outstanding years for the Cub second baseman. His figures between 1936 and 1939 included batting averages of .334, .335, .277, and .307; and hit totals of 211, 189, 173, and 191. Billy led the league in triples in 1938 with 18 and was second in doubles with 57 and in hits with 211, both in

---

[56] Bryan was a member of the House of Representatives, ran an unsuccessful campaign for President of the United States, and opposed evolution in the famous Scopes trial of 1925, where he vied with Clarence Darrow, who defended Scopes.

1936. However, in the 1938 World Series against the Bronx Bombers, Billy hit only .188 as the Yankees swept the Cubs, four games to none.

After a sub-standard offensive year in 1940, Herman was traded to the Brooklyn Dodgers early in their pennant winning 1941 season for Johnny Hudson, Charlie Gilbert, and $65,000. Along with the earlier trade of Augie Galan, this was one of the deals which started the Cubs on their decline of the 1940's that they have candidly never really recovered from, stemmed only by the 1945 pennant. Meantime, Herman actually had one of his finest offensive seasons with the 1943 Dodgers, when he batted .330 with 100 RBI's. Herman missed the 1944 and 1945 seasons to serve in World War II, but returned to play in 1946 with the Dodgers and Boston Braves (where he was traded midseason for Stew Hofferth). His swing never regained its previous form after he returned to baseball from the Navy. In his final two years, Herman hit .290 in just 137 games for the Dodgers, the Boston Braves and the Pittsburgh Pirates.

As indicated, Billy was traded prior to the 1947 season to the Pittsburgh Pirates in one of those multi-player deals so popular in those days, along with Elmer Singleton, Stan Wentzel and Whitey Wietelmann, in exchange for Bob Elliott and Hank Camelli. Herman managed the Pirates to a 61-92 record in 1947 (managing, among others, Hank Greenberg in his final major league season), and finished his playing career; that deal worked out better for the Braves and Elliott. Elliott won the 1947 NL MVP, and the Braves won the pennant in 1948.

Herman finished his career with a .304 batting average, 2345 hits, 1163 runs scored, 47 home runs (he was not a power hitter), 839 RBI and a minuscule 428 strikeouts. He played on four National League pennant winners (in 1932, 1935, and 1938 with the Cubs, and 1941 as a Dodger), but never on a World Champion. As a Cub he hit .309 (tied for 9th on the all-time team list); his 5532 Cub at-bats are 15th; and his 1712 Cub hits rank 12th all-time for the team. He hit 346 doubles as a Cub, 10th all-time.

Billy Herman still holds the National League record for most putouts in a season by a second baseman and led the league in putouts seven times. He also shares the major league record for most hits on opening day, with five, set April 14, 1936. His 666 at-bats in 1935 set the Cubs' club record for a season; it stood for 71 years until Juan Pierre broke it in 2006.

After his playing career ended, Herman then managed in the minor leagues, beginning in June 1948 with the American Association's Minneapolis Millers, then became a major league coach with the Dodgers (1952-57), Milwaukee Braves (1958-59) and Boston Red Sox (1960-64), before managing the Red Sox to mediocre records in 1965 and 1966; his 1965 Boston club lost 100 games. He coached for the California Angels (1967) and late in his career served in player development roles with the Oakland Athletics and San Diego Padres. His final record as a major league manager was 189-274 (.408).

During Herman's time with the Dodgers, he became friends with writer Ernest Hemingway, as Hemingway lived in Cuba, where the Dodgers trained in the 1940's. In Herman's words:

"Hemingway was a baseball fan. He used to come out to the park every day to watch us train. We got friendly and he invited us out to a gun club to shoot with him. They had live pigeons and clay pigeons. It was one of the few places where they had traps underground.

"He was a good shot, better than any of us. We shot with him every day for a week or 10 days until we had this safari to his house. We had dinner and we sat around and talked. He wanted to talk baseball. We were more interested in hunting. Larry French was an avid game hunter. He was interested in seeing pictures of a lion hunt--there were about a thousand of them--that Hemingway had been on.[57]

"He was one of the most interesting men I ever talked to," Herman said. "This was in March, 1942, when the war was in Burma. He had

---

[57] As we know, Hemingway was an avid outdoorsman and hunter. His novels reflect that.

covered that whole area as a newspaperman once, he said, and he told us what would happen. He said how far the Japanese would go and where they could be stopped. He was pretty much right as I recall."

Herman was elected to the Baseball Hall of Fame in 1975 by the old Veterans Committee. He died in West Palm Beach, Florida, on September 5, 1992 at the age of 83. Billy is buried in Riverside Memorial Park in Tequesta, Florida. In 2005, the park district in his hometown of New Albany, Indiana renamed the playing fields of Falling Run Park in his honor. By the way, his granddaughter, Cherie Daniels, is the wife of former Indiana governor Mitch Daniels.

There really weren't that many better players in Cub history than Billy Herman, and he was definitely in the top three second basemen they have ever had, along with Ryne Sandberg and Johnny Evers.

# 18 STAN HACK

Having an outstanding third baseman has been a recent problem for the Cubs – hopefully Kris Bryant will change that – but there are two players from the past who really stand out.

Stan Hack was most likely the second best third baseman in the history of the Cubs, with Ron Santo being the first. Hack played for the Cubs between 1932 and 1947 – the only team he played for in his career - compiled a lifetime batting average of .301, an on-base percentage of .394, and had 2193 hits to boot. He was selected to five all-star teams, and never once struck out more times than he walked – a total of 626 more walks than strikeouts over his career. He is another one of these Cub players who are not really well known by modern day fans, and he should be.

Stan Hack was a fine base runner early in his career and among the best base runners of his era. Hack led the league in stolen bases in two consecutive seasons and was an offensive weapon as a leadoff hitter before the profile for third basemen changed in the 50s, making it more of a power hitting position – think Santo, Mike Schmidt, Eddie Mathews, and Ken Boyer, for example. Defensively,

Hack was one of the best third basemen in the game for more than a decade. He was consistent, reliable, and rarely missed a game.

Hack retired at the age of 37 and went on to manage the Cubs, got remarried, and managed the Cardinals before finishing his career in professional baseball as a minor league manager. Despite growing up in California, like Gabby Hartnett, Stan Hack spent his entire adult life in Illinois where he ran a business and raised a family once his playing career was over.

Stanley Camfield Hack hit left-handed, threw right handed, stood six feet tall, and weighed 170 pounds. He was born on December 6, 1909 in Sacramento, California. After high school he worked at a bank and played semi-pro baseball on weekends. He hit .352 in his first minor league season in 1931 playing for the Sacramento Solons[58] of the Pacific Coast League, which prompted Cubs president William Veeck to personally travel to Sacramento to sign him for $40,000.[59]

Hack's major league career began in 1932 at the age of 22 with the Cubs, and he hit .236 in 72 games, appearing in the World Series (a Yankees sweep) only as a pinch runner for Gabby Hartnett in the eighth inning of Game 4. Hack played in only 20 games in 1933, spending most of his time in the International League, but he replaced Woody English at third baseman beginning in 1934, and he hit .289 in 111 games. Hack hit .311 in 124 games in 1935 as the Cubs won 21 in a row in September on their way to the NL pennant; his 14 stolen bases were good for fourth in the league, and he was third with a .406 OBP. However, he hit only .227 in the World Series against the Tigers, and was left on third base after tripling to lead off the ninth in a 3-3 game in Game Six; Detroit won the Series with a run in the bottom of the inning. His 1936 and 1937 seasons were in a

---

[58] Solons is a Greek word meaning Senators. I love the nicknames of these minor league teams!

[59] William Veeck was the father of Bill Veeck, who owned the White Sox for a time in the 50's and 60's and was a great innovator and promoter.

similar vein: 149 and 154 games played, respectively, hitting .298 and .297. In both years he finished second in the NL in stolen bases.

By this point the likeable, easygoing Hack was one of the most popular players on the Cubs and in the entire league. In a classic example of his future ingenuity, in 1935 a 21-year-old Bill Veeck – son of the Cub president - came up with a "Smile with Stan" promotion where fans were given mirrors that had Hack's picture on the reverse. Cub fans instead used the mirrors to reflect sunlight into the opposing batters' eyes, and the umpires threatened to force the Cubs to forfeit the game if the fans didn't stop. The league office, already on to Veeck for his outlandish promotions, banned any similar promotions in the future.

Hack's numbers really took off in 1938 at the age of 28, the season that climaxed with Gabby Hartnett's "Homer in the Gloamin'" against the Pirates on the way to the pennant. He hit .320 en route to leading the league in steals with 16 and finishing second in hits and runs. His performance earned him his first All-Star selection, and he finished seventh in MVP voting (the Reds' Ernie Lombardi, quite possibly the slowest man ever to play major league baseball, and who was reputedly almost thrown out at first on a ball hit off the wall, won the award). Hack hit .471 in the World Series, which resulted in another sweep by the Yankees and was the first of only two Series to be played at Wrigley Field with the ivy on the walls, its current bleacher configuration.

Hack's 1939 season was good for his second All-Star selection as he hit .298 in a career high 641 at bats; he led the league in steals for the second consecutive season and finished second in hits. His 1940 and 1941 seasons were quite similar: he hit .317 in both with 191 and 186 hits, respectively; both hit totals led the league. He was not an All-Star in 1940 but was in 1941, and he finished eighth in MVP voting in 1940. Another notable event occurred in 1940: on May 17 against the Giants at the Polo Grounds, as he led off of third base, Hack suffered a concussion after being struck by a foul ball hit by teammate Hank Leiber.

Hack hit .300 in 1942, which was the first season he did not score at least 100 runs since 1935, but his total of 91 was still good for fourth in the league, and he also finished fourth in walks and third in hits. Hack's numbers went down somewhat in 1943, when he hit .289 with an OBP 16 points greater than his slugging percentage (.384 to .366), but he still earned his fourth All Star selection. A strained relationship with manager Jimmie Wilson led Hack to "retire" at the end of the season at the age of 34, but when former teammate Charlie Grimm returned to manage the team in 1944, so did Hack, and he hit .292 in 98 games.

The last time the Chicago Cubs played host to the World Series, 1945, was also Hack's last really good season. He hit .323, good for fourth in the league, was third in on-base percentage and fifth in runs, and was selected for his fifth and final All-Star game. Teammate Phil Cavarretta won the MVP award as the Cubs won the pennant and faced the Detroit Tigers in the Series. Before Game 1 at Briggs Stadium (later renamed Tiger Stadium), Hack was seen gazing wistfully at third base, and when asked what he was looking at, he replied, "I was just looking to see if I was still standing there," in reference to his being left on third base in Game 6 of the 1935 Series.

In Game 6 of this Series, Hack doubled with two out in the bottom of the 12th inning to drive in the winning run from first base, giving the Cubs an 8-7 victory that tied the series. However, the Cubs dropped Game 7 by the score of 9-3, which remains the last World Series game they have ever played. (The controversy surrounding this game was Grimm's starting of Hank Borowy [whom the Cubs had purchased from the Yankees in late July] on very short rest after he started Game 5 three days before and had pitched in relief in Game 6 two days before); the Tigers scored five in the first inning off Borowy and cruised behind two-time AL MVP Hal Newhouser.

Hack played in 92 games in 1946, hitting .285, and his final season was the 1947 campaign, when he hit .271 in 76 games at the age of 37. At the time of his retirement, his total number of games played at third base was only 27 behind league-leading Hall of Famer Pie Traynor, and he was fourth in NL history with 1092 walks. It was not until 2001 that his career OBP among NL third basemen was surpassed by Chipper Jones of the Braves. He played 1836 games at third base for the Cubs; only Ron Santo has more games at third in franchise history.

Hack's playing career may have been over, but he quickly moved into a managerial role, leading three different minor league teams between 1948 and 1953. He replaced Cavarretta as Cubs manager for the 1954 season and led the team to a 64-90 record. This was followed by two more losing seasons: 72-81 in 1955 and 60-94 in 1956 (good for last place, 33 games behind the Dodgers).[60] He managed the Cardinals to a 3-7 mark in ten games in 1958 and finished his managerial career with a 199-272 record.

After managing three more minor league teams, Hack retired from baseball, and he died in Dixon, Illinois on December 15, 1979 at the age of 70.

Stan Hack may not have been a Hall of Famer, but his career was exemplary in many ways. He was at or near the top of single season National League leaderboards for most of his career, mostly in stolen bases, hits, runs, and walks, and, perhaps most significantly, he was a steady, consistent player for a franchise that won three pennants with him at third base.

Like many great Cubs who played before the 1960s, Hack doesn't really receive the acclaim that he should. But he was still the second best third baseman in Cub history. And Bill James, in his 'Historical Baseball Abstract (2001)', rated Stan Hack as the ninth best third baseman of All-Time.- ranked after Ron Santo and Brooks Robinson but ahead of such great players as Ken Boyer of the St. Louis Cardinals and the legendary Pie Traynor of the great Pittsburgh Pirate teams of the 1920's..

---

[60] These were really bad teams, even by Cub standards. They had a young Ernie Banks and little else.

**Smiling Stan Hack**

# 19. PHIL CAVARRETTA

If someone were to have been named "Mr. Cub" for the 1940's, that player would undoubtedly have been Phil Cavarretta. Unlike Ernie Banks, however, Phil was a native Chicagoan, and a graduate of Lane Technical High School, at that time most likely the best public school in the city of Chicago and practically a stone's throw from Wrigley Field. Cavarretta played for the Cubs for 20 seasons, a team record.

He appeared in the Cubs' last three World Series and won the National League MVP award in 1945 with an outstanding batting line of .355/.449/.500 (leading the league in both batting average and on-base percentage). While primarily a first baseman, Cavarretta never had the prototypical power expected at that position; rather it was his longevity and batting eye that carried him to stardom. He is ranked by one Cub fan website as the 11th best player in the history of the

Cubs. [61] He even managed the Cubs at the end of his career, and was Ernie Banks' first manager.

Philip Joseph Cavarretta was born on July 19, 1916 in Chicago. While attending Lane Tech, he was a local sensation as both a pitcher and hitter. Among his feats at Lane Tech were a no-hitter and eight one-hitters; he also pitched his American Legion team to a national championship in 1933.

Prior to graduation at age 17, Phil signed with the hometown Cubs; upon graduation he was assigned to the Cubs' minor league team at Peoria, making a good impression in his very first professional game on May 17, 1934 -- homering in his first at-bat and hitting for the cycle. In September, the Cubs called him up and on September 16th, he made his major league debut against the Dodgers in Brooklyn, only 18 years old. On September 26, 1934, Cavarretta made his Wrigley Field debut and got his first hit, a home run, in a 1-0 Cubs win over Cincinnati.

Before the 1935 season, Cubs' player-manager Charlie Grimm decided to focus on managing and inserted the rookie Cavarretta as the regular first baseman. Phil responded with an excellent rookie campaign at the age of 18, hitting .275 with 8 homers in 146 games. 1935 was also the year that a pair of 20-game winners, Lon Warneke and Bill Lee, led the Cubs to the World Series. Cavarretta struggled in the series, however, hitting only .125 as the Cubs lost to the Tigers four games to two.

In 1936, Phil struggled as his OBP and slugging declined, to .306 and .376 respectively in spite of a decent .273 average. After the 1936 season, the Cubs acquired first baseman Ripper Collins from the Cardinals and as a result, in 1937 Cavarretta moved to a part-time role switching between first base and the outfield. 1938 was an especially bad year as Phil hit .239 in 268 AB's. The Cubs however once again made it to the World Series. This time, Cavarretta batted .462 but the Cubs lost to the Yankees four games to none.

---

[61] www.bleedcubbieblue.com

Unfortunately, 1939 was even a worse year as on May 8, he broke his ankle and only appeared in 22 games that year. 1940 was a repeat as another broken ankle limited him to 65 games. In 1941, a healthy Cavarretta put up a solid season with a .286 average, .384 OBP and .413 slugging in 346 atbats. Due to an ear problem, Phil was exempt from military service during World War II. While many other stars left for war service, Phil remained and put up his best seasons from 1942 through 1945. Between 1942 and 1944 as a regular starter, Phil's average climbed from .270 to .291 to .321, likewise the OBP climbed from .365 to .382 to .390. In 1944, he also had a career-high 15 triples and his 197 hits tied him for the league lead.

1945 was a very good year for Cavarretta and the Cubs. Phil put up career highs in batting average (.355), on-base percentage (.449), slugging (.500) and RBI's (97). He also easily won the league MVP by over 100 points, in leading the Cubs, along with Andy Pafko and pitchers Hank Borowy and Hank Wyse, to their last World Series appearance, meeting the Tigers. Once again Cavarretta had a solid series hitting .423 but the Cubs once again lost the series, this time 4 games to 3, in their last World Series appearance, as I have already said many times.

With the National League back to full strength in 1946, Cavarretta put up solid years in 1946 and 1947 with .294 and .314 averages and .401 and .391 OBP. However, with young first baseman Eddie Waitkus back from military service, Phil once again shuttled between first base and the outfield during these years. By 1948 and 1949, Phil's days as a full time starter were over but he did put up solid years with averages of .278 and .294 respectively. By 1950, he was strictly part-time with a .273 average in 256 AB's. In all, he played 1254 games at first base, and 538 games as an outfielder, playing all three outfield positions.

1951 brought a new chapter to Cavarretta's time with the Cubs. On July 21, 1951, Cubs' manager Frankie Frisch resigned and was replaced by Cavarretta, who was team captain. The 1951 Cubs were a bad team and didn't improve under Cavarretta's leadership (27-47), finishing last. Phil did bat .311 in 206 at-bats but his playing career was essentially over. In 1952, the Cubs did improve, finishing in 5th place with a 77-77 mark, the only time between 1946 and 1963 that they did not have a losing record. That didn't last very long -- in 1953, the team regressed, falling to 7th place with a 65-89 record. On March 29, 1954, during a spring training meeting with club owner P. K. Wrigley, Cavarretta commented that he did not believe the Cubs could compete in 1954. Wrigley, not pleased with the comments, decided to fire Phil and replace him with his long-time teammate and current minor league manager Stan Hack, and offered Phil a minor league managing slot. Cavarretta quit instead of taking the Los Angeles minor league assignment and ended his association with the Cubs after 20 years. He was the first manager ever replaced during spring training. Incidentally, Phil was right: the 1954 team could not compete (like virtually every other team between 1946 and 1963) -- they finished with a 64-90 record, their fourth 90+ loss season since 1948. See what happens when you tell your boss something that is absolutely true but that he or she does not want to hear!

After leaving the Cubs, Phil signed with the cross-town Chicago White Sox in May 1954 as a utility player. He batted .316 in 158 AB's for the Sox in 1954. As the 1955 season started, Cavarretta was once again a member of the Sox as a utility player. However, he had only four at-bats, and was released on May 9th, ending his major league career. He remained in baseball as a coach, scout and manager well into the 1970's, coaching for the Tigers in the 1960's, and working as a minor league batting instructor for the Mets in the 1970's.

In addition to his 20 years as a major league baseball player, Cavarretta even played a game of ping pong against actress Betty Grable in 1935 at spring training on Catalina, telling an interviewer in 2007, "And you know what, she was pretty good! I had to really concentrate to beat her, so all the guys wouldn't get on me. But I was tricky when I played — I'd put a little slice on the ball, give it some 'English' — it was the only way I could stay close to her! But that was the last time I saw her." (Maybe he spent too much time looking at her famous legs to pay attention to ping pong.)

In case you have not heard of Betty Grable, she was an actress and singer, and the most popular pinup girl for the American servicemen during World War II.

**Betty Grable in the most famous pinup photo of all time. Taken during World War II. I didn't know she played ping pong!**

Phil Cavarretta died in December 2013 at the age of 94 in Lilburn, Georgia. One grandson, Jeffrey Brown, of Lubbock, Texas, told the AP that he was one of several family members who grew up as baseball players largely because of Cavarretta."We're full of sorrow, but he lived a full, wonderful life," Brown said.

Cavarretta ranks in the top ten in many categories on the Cubs all-time lists: sixth in games played (1953), tenth in at bats (6592), tenth in runs (968), tenth in hits (1927), tenth in RBI's (896) and seventh in walks (794). His lifetime batting average was .293 and he played in three World Series – 1935, 1938, and 1945. His .371 OBA ranks thirteenth in Cub history -- not bad for a kid from Lane Tech.

# 20. ERNIE BANKS

Ernie Banks is, was, and always will be, my favorite Chicago Cub player – it's as simple as that. When I was growing up in the 1950's, he was far and away the best player on the Cubs, about the only shining light on an otherwise dismal team throughout the decade. Plus, he was just a wonderful fellow, treated the fans with great respect, and just loved to play the game of baseball. His legendary comment of "Let's play two today!" was remembered by many at his recent funeral. Most importantly, he was probably the best Chicago Cub player of all time, with all due apologies to Cap Anson. And he was the first one of these players that I actually saw play, having been born in 1947.[62]

**Mr Cub – Ernie Banks – my all time favorite player – in 1970**

Ernie Banks came to the Cubs from the Kansas City Monarchs of the Negro League at the tail end of 1953, along with Gene Baker, when I was 6 years old. He remained with the Cubs until 1971, when he retired at the age of 40. He was the one Cub player who spanned my

---

[62] Hank Sauer was actually my first Cub hero, but that was relatively short lived.

entire youth, from age 6 until I was 24. And he was one of a trio of great black players who were brought into the National League at roughly the same time, the others being Willie Mays and Henry Aaron, of course, who contributed to the National League dominating the all-star game for a period of many years. When I played wiffle ball with my friend, he was a Cardinal fan and was always Stan Musial, while I was always Ernie Banks. I even tried to emulate that Banks swing – bat straight up in the air, fingers constantly moving on the bat, using his wrists to propel those home runs.

"My life is like a miracle," Banks said a few years ago. A power-hitting shortstop ahead of his time – in those days, shortstops were slick fielding, no-hit players - he won back-to-back MVP awards in 1958 and '59, staking a lasting claim as arguably the greatest player in Cubs history. In 1959, for example, the Cubs finished fifth out of eight teams in the National League with a record of 74-80, 13 games out of first place; but without Banks, they would have finished last, no question about that.

Ernest Banks was born in Dallas, Texas, to Eddie and Essie Banks on January 31, 1931. He had eleven siblings, ten of them younger. His father, who had worked in construction and was a warehouse loader for a grocery chain, played baseball for black semi-pro teams in Texas. As a child, Banks was not very interested in baseball, preferring swimming, basketball and football. His father bought him a baseball glove for less than three dollars at the local Woolworth-type store and then bribed Banks with nickels and dimes to play catch. Ernie's mother encouraged him to follow one of his grandfathers into a career as a minister. Thank God for Cub fans he did not listen to his mother's advice on this one!

Banks had picked cotton as a boy, helping to support his family by hiring himself out as a field hand for farmers east of Dallas. He believes that's where he developed the strong, quick hands he used to create his niche in baseball.

"My hitting was just the way I did it," Banks said."I picked cotton. I don't know if you know anything about this. I picked cotton when I was quite young. My dad used to take me to the cotton fields, tell me

142

to pick cotton. It taught me how to use my hands. I would grab. When I started to play baseball I just had the natural quick hands. That was my extra advantage, my slight edge over anybody else. I had quick hands. I could wait to the last minute and hit the ball. Nobody could understand it. But I had those quick hands, which I developed by picking cotton."[63]

Ernie Banks graduated from Booker T. Washington High School in Dallas in 1950. He was an outstanding athlete and lettered in basketball, football, and track. While the school did not have a baseball team, he played fastpitch softball for a church team during the summer. He was also a member of the Amarillo Colts, a semipro baseball team. History professor Timothy Gilfoyle wrote that Banks was discovered by Bill Blair, a family friend who scouted for the Kansas City Monarchs of the Negro American League. Other sources report that he was noticed by former Negro League star Cool Papa Bell of the Monarchs.

In 1951, Banks was drafted into the US Army and served in Germany during the Korean War. He suffered a knee injury in basic training, but recovered after a few weeks of rest and therapy. He served as a flag bearer in the 45th Anti-Aircraft Artillery Battalion at Fort Bliss and while there he played with the Harlem Globetrotters on a part-time basis. In 1953, he was discharged from the army and finished playing for the Monarchs that season with a .347 batting average.

Even at that young age, Ernie Banks loved playing baseball. Banks told reporters he was having so much fun riding buses with the Kansas City Monarchs that he wasn't happy when owner Tom Baird sold him and pitcher Bill Dickey – not to be confused with the great Yankee catcher Bill Dickey - to the Cubs for $20,000 in September, 1953. Yet when Banks pulled on one of the Cubs' white flannel uniforms, he hit the first pitch he saw in batting practice over the ivy-covered wall. It was like he was hand-delivered to be, in the words of documentarian Ken Burns, "the sort of spice in this gumbo called the Chicago Cubs, beloved by everybody, embraced by everybody."

---

[63] www.sportsonearth.com – article by Phil Rogers

It was never as easy as Banks made it look, right from that first swing, but he made it look so easy. "I just stepped into the batting cage," Banks said. "They threw me the ball, boom, I hit it out of the park ... Is that all there is?"[64]

As well as anyone in baseball history, Banks rolled with the punches. He was 22 when he arrived at Wrigley Field and played 19 seasons there. He batted .274, hit 512 home runs and played in 14 All-Star games in his career, always while living far away from his white teammates because of Chicago's housing restrictions. His two best years were 1958, when he went .313 with 47 home runs and 129 runs batted in, and 1959, when he went .304, 45, and 143; he won the Most Valuable Player award both years and was probably the best player in either league those two years. As I have said, the Cubs finished fifth in the league out of eight teams in 1959 with a record of 74-80, and would certainly have been last without him. Players from 5$^{th}$ place teams don't usually win the MVP, but that's how good Mr. Cub was.

I firmly believe that Banks did a lot for improving race relations in Chicago. He was a favorite of fans of all colors because of his personality as well as his skills. "I tried to sign every kid's autograph," Banks said. "Because in my mind I thought that one day I might have to ask this kid for a job." I remember him signing one for me one time.

Banks was a very good but not outstanding defensive shortstop. He was very sure handed but did not have the range of a truly great shortstop like Luis Aparicio of the White Sox, for example. Knee injuries eventually forced Banks to move from shortstop to first base in 1962, after an unsuccessful trial in left field. He remained at first base for the remainder of his career and was a very good first baseman.

When the Cubs grew competitive in the late 1960s under Leo Durocher, Banks and fellow Hall of Famer Billy Williams were living

---

[64] Referencing the Peggy Lee song by the same name – Is That All There Is?

on the South Side. Chicago was the scene of race riots in 1966, '67 and '68, and organizers were always trying to pull Banks into one movement or another. He resisted direct involvement, instead showing up to the ballpark with a good attitude every day. I am guessing that, just by his easygoing personality, he did more to improve race relations in Chicago than just about anybody.

"Well", he told them, "I don't have time to march but I contribute voluntarily," said fellow Hall of Famer Monte Irvin of Ernie; Irvin played alongside Banks on the 1956 Cubs. "'I try to play good baseball to make up for it that way. Give the kids somebody to look up to, so the fans come to the ballpark pleased.' That's what he thought. I think that's a pretty good attitude."

Durocher, who was jealous of Banks' popularity, looked to a variety of players to replace Banks at first - Lee Thomas, John Boccabella, John Herrnstein, Clarence Jones and others, but every year Banks would prove he belonged in the middle of the lineup. He hit 23 homers and drove in 106 runs at age 38 in 1969, when Gil Hodges' Mets got hot down the stretch and overtook the Cubs, and in the process broke the hearts of millions in Chicago, including mine.[65]

Banks refused to be baited into confrontations, even by Durocher. Whenever Durocher would take Banks out of the lineup, the franchise icon would make a point to sit next to his manager in the dugout. "When somebody resented me, didn't like me -- and that was the case with Leo -- I kind of killed them with kindness," Banks said. "On the bench, I'd always sit beside him, on the plane sit beside him, in the dugout sit beside him. He's always looking around and seeing me ... When you light a fire under my heels, it just made me better." Banks, of course, was known for "Let's play two," and various other catch phrases that rolled off his tongue. He was a chatterbox throughout his life -- Irvin recalls Pee Wee Reese saying the Cubs never won because Banks "talked 'em to death" -- but rarely talked

---

[65] In fairness to Durocher, who could be quite a jerk, Banks was nowhere near the player he once was by the time Durocher got to Chicago. But Leo made great beer commercials. "How about another Schlitz, fellas?" he would say to reporters during the commercial.

about the difficulties he faced in life, especially discrimination early in his career.

Banks certainly had an interesting personal life, including being married four times. He married his first wife Mollye Ector in 1953. He had proposed to her in a letter from Germany and they married when he returned to the U.S. He filed for divorce two years later. The couple briefly reconciled in early 1959. By that summer, they agreed on a divorce settlement that would pay $65,000 to Ector in lieu of alimony. Shortly thereafter, Banks eloped with Eloyce Johnson. Within a year, the couple had twin sons, who both spoke eloquently at his funeral, by the way. They had a daughter four years after that.

A lifelong Republican – now there's a surprise! - Banks ran for alderman in Chicago in 1963. He lost the election and later said, "People knew me only as a baseball player. They didn't think I qualified as a government official and no matter what I did I couldn't change my image. ... What I learned, was that it was going to be hard for me to disengage myself from my baseball life and I would have to compensate for it after my playing days were over." [66]

Ernie was always into self-improvement. In 1966, Banks worked for Seaway National Bank in the offseason and enrolled in a banking correspondence course. He bought into several business ventures during his playing career, including a gas station. Though he had been paid modestly in comparison to other baseball stars, Banks had taken the advice of Cub owner P.K. Wrigley and invested much of his earnings. He later spent time working for an insurance company and for New World Van Lines. Banks began building assets that would be worth an estimated $4 million by the time he was 55 years old. (Many athletes waste their money and are penniless when they retire – obviously, Banks was not one of them.)

Banks and Bob Nelson became the first black owners of a U.S. Ford Motor Company dealership in 1967. Nelson had been the first non-white commissioned officer in the United States Army Air Forces

---

[66] Remember, Chicago is a very Democratic city, so even Ernie Banks could not win as a Republican.

during World War II; he operated an import car dealership before the venture with Banks. Banks was then appointed to the board of directors of the Chicago Transit Authority in 1969. On a trip to Europe, Banks was able to visit the Pope, who presented him with a medal that became a proud possession.

Banks was divorced from Eloyce in 1981. She received several valuable items from his playing career as part of their divorce settlement, including his 500th home run ball. She sold the items not long after the divorce. In 1984, he married a woman named Marjorie. In 1993, Marjorie was part of a group that met with MLB executives about race relations in baseball after allegations of racial slurs surfaced against Cincinnati Reds owner Marge Schott. They divorced, and Banks married Liz Ellzey in 1997, with Hank Aaron serving as his best man. In late 2008, Banks and Ellzey adopted an infant daughter.

Ernie Banks was voted into the National Baseball Hall of Fame in 1977, his first year of eligibility – wow, there's a surprise! He received votes on 321 of the 383 ballots. Though several players were selected through the Veterans Committee and the Special Committee on the Negro Leagues that year, Banks was the only player elected by the Baseball Writers' Association of America. He was inducted on August 8 of that year. During his induction speech, Banks said, "We've got the setting – sunshine, fresh air, the team behind us. So let's play two!"

The Cubs retired Banks' uniform number 14 in 1982. Not surprisingly, he was the first Cub player to have his number retired by the team – were you surprised it was not Harry Chiti? No other numbers were retired by the team for another five years, when Billy Williams received the honor. Through the 2014 season, only six former Cubs, along with Brooklyn Dodger Jackie Robinson, have had their numbers retired by the organization.. He was employed as the corporate sales representative for the Cubs at the time of the ceremony.

There were some problems with Ernie as a team ambassador – he was so interested in pleasing people, he would double schedule himself and not show up to certain events, obviously. Once the Cubs took charge of his schedule, there were no more problems.

At the 1990 Major League Baseball All-Star Game, the first one held at Wrigley Field since Banks' playing days, he threw out the ceremonial first pitch to starting catcher Mike Scioscia. Ernie was named to the Major League Baseball All-Century Team in 1999. In the same year, the Society for American Baseball Research listed him 27th on a list of the 100 greatest baseball players. I can't say I disagree with that.

Banks was also involved in many charitable activities through the years that often went unnoticed. And on March 31, 2008, a statue of Banks ("Mr. Cub") was unveiled in front of Wrigley Field – see photo on page 6. In 2009, Banks was named a Library of Congress Living Legend, a designation that recognizes those "who have made significant contributions to America's diverse cultural, scientific and social heritage." On August 8, 2013, he was announced as a recipient of the Presidential Medal of Freedom. Banks was honored with 15 other people, including Bill Clinton and Oprah Winfrey. He said that he presented President Obama with a bat that belonged to Jackie Robinson.

Banks died of a heart attack at a Chicago hospital on January 23, 2015, shortly before his 84th birthday. Frankly, I thought he would live forever, but of course, that is ridiculous. Reactions and tributes were widespread. Chicago Mayor Rahm Emanuel said in a statement: "Ernie Banks was more than a baseball player. He was one of Chicago's greatest ambassadors. He loved this city as much as he loved — and lived for — the game of baseball." President Barack Obama – a White Sox fan who never hides his dislike of the Cubs - and his wife, Michelle, called Banks "an incredible ambassador for baseball, and for the city of Chicago." President Obama hailed his "cheer and his optimism and his eternal faith that someday the Cubs would go all the way." Finally, outgoing Commissioner Bud Selig, on his final day in office, posted this tribute through social media:

"Ernie Banks was synonymous with a childlike enthusiasm for baseball. It was not just great talent but also his relentless spirit of

148

optimism that made him a back-to-back National League MVP, a Hall of Famer, a member of our All-Century Team, a recipient of the Presidential Medal of Freedom and, indeed, forever 'Mr. Cub.' His joyous outlook will never be forgotten by fans of the Cubs and all those who love Baseball."

All you need to know about Ernie Banks can be summed up in the following story. I was listening to radio station WSCR The SCORE the day after Ernie Banks died. The host was asking callers to call in and give their feelings about Ernie Banks. The first caller stated as follows, and I paraphrase here:

"I am a lifelong White Sox fan and like most Sox fans, I have no use for the Cubs. But my feelings toward Ernie Banks are quite different. A few years ago, my 19-year-old son was dying of brain cancer – he has since passed away. A friend of mine, who knew Ernie Banks, told Banks about my son. Ernie drove from Chicago to my son's hospital in Valparaiso, Indiana and spent the entire afternoon with my son. They talked about baseball, sports, and life in general. It ended up being the best day of my son's life since he was diagnosed with cancer. And I can't thank Ernie Banks enough for what he did for my son that day."

That's really all you need to know about Mr. Cub, Ernie Banks. Ernie Banks has always been my favorite baseball player, and that will never change.

**Mr. Cub – Ernie Banks – naturally, a smile on his face**

# 21 RON SANTO

If Ernie Banks is my all-time favorite Cub player, Ron Santo is 1A. Ron Santo may well be the best third baseman in Chicago Cub history, and is rated by one service – ESPN – as the second greatest player in Cub history, behind Ernie Banks of course, with Cap Anson third. He is also beloved by most Cub fans from 1960 on because of his unending passion for the team during his tenure as the Cubs' radio analyst, and for the physical trials and tribulations he went through during his life because of diabetes.

Ron Santo played for the Cubs from 1960 through 1973 before having one final and unfulfilling year with the White Sox in 1974. For most of that time, he was the Cubs' cleanup hitter, with Billy Williams batting third and Ernie Banks batting fifth. They formed a powerful 3-4-5 combination which made baseball on the north side of Chicago always interesting and sometimes even successful.

**Ron Santo in the on-deck circle**

Ron Santo was a nine-time All Star, led the league in walks four times, lead the league in on base percentage twice, and was in the top ten in runs batted in seven times.

He personified the Chicago Cubs for more than 50 years as a player, a broadcaster and an icon. His legend remains vibrant, a living monument to his love for the game and his courage while fighting a debilitating disease.

Ronald Edward Santo was born on Feb. 25, 1940, in Seattle, Washington. Santo grew up to be a talented multi-sport amateur athlete. He began to attract the attention of big league scouts in 1958 as a catcher, and he signed with the Cubs in 1959.

For Santo, there was much adversity throughout his life. His father was an alcoholic who left the family when Santo and his sister were youngsters. His mother remarried, and then in 1973, when his mother and stepfather were driving from California to see him at spring training in Arizona, both were killed in an auto accident.

Because of his agility, Santo was moved from catcher to third base and immediately made an impact in the minors, hitting .327 with 87 RBI for Double-A San Antonio in 1959. The next season, Santo had 32 RBI in 71 games with Triple-A Houston before getting the call to the majors. When he first entered Wrigley Field, walking alongside Ernie Banks, he was transfixed.

"We came out of the clubhouse in left field, and I'm walking down on the grass and I'm looking out to the outfield, and the ivy hadn't quite blossomed yet, but it was close," he told The Denver Post in 2004. "It was like walking on air. There was a feeling of electricity that I've never had."

In his June 26, 1960 debut against the Pirates, Santo had three hits and five RBI in a double-header sweep. He never appeared in another minor league game.

Santo finished fourth in the National League Rookie of the Year vote that season despite appearing in only 95 games. The next season,

Santo firmly entrenched himself at third base by hitting 23 home runs and driving in 83 runs.

But all the while, Santo was harboring a secret that no one in the Cub organization knew anything about. During a routine physical at age 18, just before his minor league career began, doctors diagnosed Santo with Type 1 juvenile diabetes. At the time, the life expectancy of a juvenile diabetic was thought to be about 25 years.

"I didn't know what it was, so I went to the library and looked it up," he told The Chicago Sun-Times in 1990. "I can still remember the feeling I had when I read the description: life expectancy of a juvenile insulin-dependent diabetic: 25 years. It also stated that it would cause blindness, kidney failure and hardening of the arteries. At that point, I said to myself, 'I'm going to fight this thing and beat it.' That's how badly I wanted to live and be a big league ballplayer."

So Ron Santo educated himself about the disease and taught himself how to administer insulin injections. Santo kept his secret from the Cubs until he was named to his first All-Star team in 1963, fearing that management's knowledge of his illness might have damaged his career. He did not allow the public to know of his diabetes until 1971.

Diabetes did not stop him from becoming a great player. He was named to his first All-Star Game in 1963, and won the first of five straight Gold Glove Awards in 1964. From 1963-70, Santo averaged almost 29 homers and 106 RBI per season. He also led the NL in walks four times between 1964 and 1968, and paced the league in on-base percentage twice in that same span.

Santo was a part of a core group of players – including Hall of Famers Ernie Banks, Ferguson Jenkins and Billy Williams – who led the Cubs back into contention in the late 1960s. In 1969, the Cubs paced the newly created NL East for most of the season before fading in September as the Miracle Mets clinched the title. It would be Santo's best chance at a postseason appearance that would never come. As a fan, I can remember the joyous ride to the top of the NL

East that lasted until mid August, and the awful feeling after that as the New York Mets got hot just as the Cubs went cold.

Santo made the All-Star team nine times between 1961 and 73, but by 1973, the 33-year-old Santo was entering the twilight of his career, with the Cubs slowly dismantling the great core of their 1960s teams. Following the 1973 season – where he hit 20 home runs and drove in 77 runs – Santo became the first player to invoke the new 10-and-5 rule, designed to allow players with 10 years in the big leagues and the last five with the same team, to veto trades. The Cubs tried to trade Santo to the Angels, but Santo rejected it. He later accepted a deal to the cross-town White Sox. 1974 would be his last year as a player.

Ron finished his career with a .277 average, 342 home runs, 1,331 RBI, 1,108 walks and 1,138 runs scored. As good as he was on offense, he was even better defensively. Santo led all NL third basemen in putouts seven times, assists seven times and total chances nine times – and retired with NL records for most assists in a season by a third baseman, most double plays by a third baseman in a career and most chances accepted at third base. Although he was slow on the basepaths, Santo was amazingly quick at third base.

**Ron Santo with teammate and buddy Glenn Beckert, receiving one of his five Gold Gloves**

## Life after His Playing Career Was Over

Santo entered the business world during his playing career and after retiring following the 1974 season. What Cub fan can forget Ron Santo Pizza and a collection of chicken and other restaurants that bore his name? But he returned to the Cubs in 1990 as a radio broadcaster, first with Harry Caray and then with Pat Hughes - quickly winning over a new generation of fans with his unabashed support of the team. Despite numerous illnesses – including heart bypass surgery and bladder cancer – Santo rarely missed work, even after having both legs amputated due to his diabetic condition.

He and Pat Hughes, in particular, were terrific as a team in the radio booth. To be frank, Santo was not the best analyst in baseball by a long shot – compared to someone like Steve Stone who excels in that role – but the chemistry between the Santo and Hughes made them a great team and made listening to them an enjoyable experience. I just think of the famous Brant Brown dropped fly ball on September 23, 1998 – you can hear Pat Hughes describing the play and Ron Santo screaming, "Oh, no!" as Brown dropped what should have been an easy game-ending catch. Or during the singing of the National Anthem at Shea Stadium, Pat Hughes smelling something burning in the broadcast booth and turning around to find that Santo's toupee had gotten too close to one of the heaters and caught fire. Just priceless!

After his playing days ended, Santo raised millions of dollars, perhaps hundreds of millions of dollars, for diabetes research. His walks to raise funds for JDRF – the Juvenile Diabetes Research Fund – are legendary in the Chicago area. And personally, the disease took a heavy toll on him. He had heart attacks, went through quadruple-bypass surgery, then underwent amputation of his legs, in 2001 and 2002, as a result of circulatory problems. But Ron Santo kept going until the very end. Using prostheses and walking with a cane, he persevered as a broadcaster, elated when things went right and deflated when the Cubs were, well, the Cubs.

The Cubs retired his No. 10 at Wrigley Field in September 2003, and he stood and waved from the radio booth as the crowd cheered.

When the Cubs had first announced they would fly Santo's number from the left-field foul pole, he told The Associated Press: "There's nothing more important to me in my life than this happening to me. I'm a Cubbie. I'll always be a Cubbie." That meant as much or more to him than being elected to baseball's Hall of Fame. He was finally elected to the HOF by the Veterans' Committee in 2012, roughly a year after his death.

Ron Santo passed away on December 3, 2010, at the age of 70. The cause was complications of bladder cancer. Santo was survived by his wife, Vicki; four children; and his grandchildren.

As far as tributes to Santo are concerned, *This Old Cub* is a very moving documentary film which was released in 2004. The film is centered on Ron Santo and both his playing days and his battle against diabetes. The film was written, co-produced, and directed by Santo's son Jeff, a documentary film producer.

Ernie Banks was known as Mr. Cub. Nonetheless, as Billy Williams once put it: "If you say Chicago Cubs, you say Ron Santo." Chicago Cub fans will always love Ron Santo, and rightly so.

**Ron Santo, kicking off one of his walks for JDRF.**

## 22 BILLY WILLIAMS

Billy Williams is rated by one source – www.bleedcubbieblue.com - as the fifth best player in Chicago Cubs history. After watching him play the game for 15 years, I can't say that I disagree with that assessment.

"Sweet swinging" Billy Williams – the pride of Whistler, Alabama - had such a beautiful, natural swing – the best left-handed swing since Ted Williams, according to many. It's no wonder he was such a good hitter and one of the best players in Chicago Cub history.

He approached the game in a quiet manner, consistently producing year in and year out, literally never missing a game for years, playing in 1117 consecutive games from 1963 through 1970 (a then-NL record, eventually broken by Steve Garvey). He played in 150 or more games for twelve straight seasons, 1962-1973, and, along with Ron Santo, is the co-club record holder for games in a season, 164 (all the decisions plus two tie games in 1965); only one man, Maury Wills, has ever played in more regular-season games in a year, and it took a three-game playoff against the Giants in 1962 to do that). Williams had a unique approach at the plate, the big blue number 26 on his back, in that left-hand batter's box at Wrigley Field, bat standing almost straight up and down, then whipping with amazing bat speed to send another rope of a line drive down the right-field line, or into the bleachers. Williams also hit quite a few opposite field home runs to left field, as opposed to Ernie Banks, who may have never hit a homer to right field.

Billy Leo Williams was born on June 15, 1938 in Whistler, Alabama. These are facts known to every Cub fan of my generation, because TV announcer Jack Brickhouse[67] used to remind us of them constantly. He was signed in 1956 out of high school, and began playing in the Cubs' minor league system. In 1959, playing at the Double-A level in San Antonio, Williams got homesick, jumped the team, and went home to Alabama.

Buck O'Neil, another pioneer black player and coach, then a scout for the Cubs, went to visit Billy. Although O'Neil hadn't been the one personally responsible for signing Williams, he knew of Billy's talent and thought he could become a major league star. In his wonderful book *I Was Right On Time*, O'Neil describes how he got Williams to return to play in Texas:

"I hadn't signed Billy, but I had gotten to know him and his family pretty well during his first year of pro ball in Class D. So when I showed up at his parents' home, I was as friendly as could be. I shook hands all around, making out like it was just a social call. I said nothing about Billy jumping the team. We chatted for a while, then I took them all out to dinner."

"The next night his mother fixed dinner, and after the table was cleared, I said to Billy, "C'mon. Let's go out to the ballyard. There's a

---

[67] Jack Brickhouse broadcasted Cub games on WGN from 1940 until 1981, until they decided they wanted a younger look, so they replaced Jack with Harry Caray, who was actually older than Brickhouse!

player I want you to see." This was just a pretense, of course, although you never knew what you might find in Mobile, the home of great players like Henry Aaron and Willie McCovey. "When we got to the ballpark -- it was just a little sandlot league -- Billy was mobbed by the younger ballplayers." 'Billy, we hear you're doin' great.' 'Billy, have you met Ernie Banks?' 'Billy, what brings you home?'"

"The kids treated him like a superstar, and I could see that Billy enjoyed the attention. I spent five days in Mobile with the Williams family, and I never said one word about him going back to San Antonio. I never had to. What sold him was those other hungry young ballplayers. He saw what a great thing he had going, and he knew that if he blew it, there were a hundred guys waiting in line to take his place."

"Out of the blue one day, Billy said, 'I think I'm ready to go back.' I called the office to give John Holland [the Cubs' GM] the news, and he said, 'Put him on a bus and send him back to Texas.' I said, 'I'm not putting him on any bus. I'm putting him in my car and driving him to San Antonio.' On our way to Texas we talked about a lot of things. It seems that in addition to being homesick, he was having a little crisis of confidence. I told him one day he was going to be right up there with Ernie Banks and the other big stars. 'Do you really think so?' he said. 'I know so,' I said. Sure enough, Billy Williams is right up there with Ernie Banks -- in Cooperstown.[68]

With that vote of confidence, and having gotten some coaching help at San Antonio from Hall of Famer Rogers Hornsby, Williams made it to Chicago in the late summer of 1959 at the age of 21. He made his major league debut on August 6, in an otherwise unremarkable 4-2 Cub win over the Phillies. He hit only .152 that year, and a little better -- .277/.346/.489 -- in 47 at-bats in 1960, including his first

---

[68] John (Buck) O'Neil managed the Kansas City Monarchs of the Negro League and was the first African-American coach in major league baseball. He died in 2006, just a month short of his 95th birthday. Baseball and the Chicago Cubs owe him a lot!

major league home run, off another Williams, Stan of the Dodgers, on October 1, 1960 at the Los Angeles Coliseum.

In 1961, at the age of 23, Billy was installed as the Cubs' regular left fielder. The team was terrible – remember, this is the Cubs, so that should be no surprise - as they finished 64-90 and would have finished last if not for the even more awful Phillies -- but Billy blossomed. He hit .278/.338/.484 with 25 HR and 86 RBI, and was named National League Rookie of the Year, the first of two straight Cub Rookies of the Year - (the late Kenny Hubbs being the next, in 1962).[69]

The following year Billy began a remarkable streak -- no, not his consecutive game streak, but a series of twelve straight years in which he would drive in no fewer than 84 runs, and in ten of those years (all except 1967 and 1973) he had 90 or more. He was primarily a left fielder, although in 1965 and 1966, he played mostly in right field. He didn't really have the arm or the range to cover right field -- he played there mostly because the other options, guys like Doug Clemens, Don Landrum and Byron Browne were even worse (with players like that, is it any wonder the Cubs were awful?) -- and so in 1967 he moved back to left field, to stay there until an ill-advised attempt to make him a first baseman in 1974.

On September 21, 1963, Billy sat out an otherwise ordinary 4-0 loss to the Braves -- Warren Spahn was pitching, and perhaps Bob Kennedy sat him against "a tough lefty". It would be the last game he would miss for nearly seven years. The next day, Billy began a consecutive-game playing streak that lasted until September 3, 1970, when Billy told manager Leo Durocher he wanted to end the streak -- it had gotten too big for him, he thought, and he didn't want the added pressure as he approached what was then the second-longest streak in history, Everett Scott's 1307 games; the streak had been kept going the previous year in mid-June with three token pinch-hitting appearances after he had suffered a minor injury in Cincinnati.

---

[69] Ken Hubbs was killed in a private plane crash in February of 1964, at the age of 22. He may very well have ended up being a Hall of Famer, he had that much promise.

Billy's National League record was broken by Steve Garvey on April 16, 1983. Interesting note: had Williams not skipped that September 1963 game, his streak would have been 166 games longer (1283), as he had played in all 155 previous games that year, and the final 11 games of 1962.

One of Billy's biggest disappointments was never winning a MVP award, even in his two biggest years, 1970 and 1972. In 1970, a hitters' year, he hit .322/.391/.586, with 42 HR and 129 RBI. He led the National League in runs, hits (tied with Pete Rose) and total bases, but lost the MVP to Johnny Bench, who had a spectacular year for the eventual pennant-winners, the Reds. Two years later, it was the same story -- Billy won the batting title (the first Cub to do so since Phil Cavarretta in 1945) with a .333 average; the rest of his line included a .398 OBA, a .606 SLG, and finishing second in runs batted in (by two) and third in homers (by three) -- to Bench, who again won the MVP. That's about as close as anyone has come to winning the Triple Crown in the last 45 years. Billy also led the league in 1972 in total bases, slugging percentage, OPS and extra-base hits. During one 12-game stretch in mid-July 1972, Billy went 28-for-53 (.528) with 6 HR and 17 RBI. Meanwhile, the Cubs finished second both years.

But the Cubs and Cubs fans had given their own recognition to Billy three years earlier; on June 29, 1969, the Cubs held "Billy Williams Day" at Wrigley Field, the day that Billy broke Stan Musial's NL record for consecutive games (895). With the Cubs flying high in the NL East at the time, it is possible that more people were either in Wrigley Field or attempted to get in, than on any other day in history. The announced attendance was 41,060, but contemporary estimates said that perhaps as many as 50,000 people were turned away at the gate.

At the end of the 1973 season, the Cubs "backed up the truck" and dealt away so many of the stars the fans thought were going to win it all for the club, including Ran Santo, Fergie Jenkins, Randy Hundley, and Glenn Beckert. (Pitchers Bill Hands and Ken Holtzman were already gone). Billy was one of those who survived the initial purge, but was unhappy because the new manager, Jim Marshall, tried to play him at first base, a position he had played only briefly before 1974. The Cubs sunk to a 96-loss depth and Billy was traded to the Oakland A's shortly after the 1974 season ended, for Darold Knowles, Bob Locker, and Manny Trillo.

At Oakland, Billy was one of the first veteran stars to be used as a fulltime designated hitter. Though he hit only .244 in 1975, he hit 23 HR and drove in 81 runs, including his 400th career HR on June 12, 1975 in Milwaukee, a game which featured a HR from a 400-HR player (Williams) and a 700-HR player (Henry Aaron) -- and it was also the first home run Aaron hit in Milwaukee as a Brewer. The A's won the AL West that year, and Billy Williams became the only position player among the famed 1969 crew (Kenny Holtzman was the only pitcher) to play in the postseason. Unfortunately, he didn't do very well -- going 0-for-7 -- and he retired as a player after the following year.

Over an 18-season big league career (1959-76), 16 spent with the Cubs, Williams had 2,711 hits, a .290 batting average, 426 home runs, hit 20 or more home runs 13 straight seasons, and once held the National League record for consecutive games played with 1,117.

"Billy Williams is the best hitter, day-in and day-out, that I have ever seen," said longtime Cubs teammate Don Kessinger. "He's unbelievable. He didn't hit for just one or two days, or one or two weeks. He hit all the time."

But even in his autobiography Williams acknowledged the perception of his less-than-flashy career, writing, "People say I'm not an exciting player. I go out there and catch the ball and hit the ball and play the game like it should be played."

A longtime opponent, Joe Torre, explained, "He leads his club with his bat and just the way he plays. I think he knows if he blows his stack, he might affect a lot of the young kids, and Billy feels that kind of responsibility to his teammates, and it carries over."

Fellow Hall of Famer Lou Boudreau, a one-time Cubs broadcaster, said, "If he's worried, he never shows it. It helps him mentally at the plate. I don't think he allows outside matters to affect him once that game gets underway."

Though Williams may have been overshadowed, he was not unrecognized, with six All-Star Game selections, the NL Rookie of the Year Award in 1961, and The Sporting News Player of the Year in 1972, when, as noted, he led the league with a .333 batting average while also hitting 37 home runs and driving in 122 runs.

Billy Williams coached for the Cubs in varying capacities (mainly as first base and bench coach) for fifteen seasons after his retirement as a player, also spending three years in Oakland as an A's coach in the mid-1980's. The thirty-one seasons in which he wore the Cub uniform are more than any other single individual.

Billy Williams has resided in the Chicago area since he retired from baseball. He was often mentioned as possible managerial material, but was never seriously considered; I guess people thought he was too easygoing to be a manager. He did resent that a bit, but in typical Billy Williams fashion, he did not make a big deal of it.

Billy Williams was enshrined in the Baseball Hall of Fame in 1987 after receiving 86 percent of the votes. The first line of text on Billy Williams' National Baseball Hall of Fame plaque may sum up the longtime Chicago Cub leftfielder the best: "Soft-spoken, clutch performer was one of the most respected hitters of his day."

"The leader of the Cubs is, of all people, the quiet man of the clubhouse, Billy Williams," wrote Chicago sports columnist Bill Gleason. "Billy Williams, who seldom speaks in a voice that can be heard beyond his own cubicle, who wouldn't say 'Rah! Rah!' if (Cubs owner) Phil Wrigley promised him a $10,000 bonus for each 'Rah!' is the man to whom the Cubs look for leadership."

Gleason continued. "He combines the dignity of Ernie Banks, the determination of (Ron) Santo, and the competitive fires of (Randy) Hundley, and he plays every day, every night."

That pretty much says it all.

**Billy Williams – in the top 5 of all-time Cubs**

# 23 FERGIE JENKINS

Fergie Jenkins was the ace of the Cub pitching staff during the mid 60's through early 70's. Between 1967 and 1974, Fergie won 20 or more games seven out of eight years, and six years in a row between 1967 and 1972 – all six years with the Cubs. He was a true ace, and one of the best pitchers in baseball during that period. He is also one of only four pitchers – Greg Maddux is one of the other three[70] – with 3,000 or more strikeouts and fewer than 1,000 walks. [71]

While he pitched for the Philadelphia Phillies, Texas Rangers, and Boston Red Sox, Fergie is best known for his tenure with the Cubs from 1966-1973. In 1982-1983, he finished his career in a return stint with the Cubs.

---

[70] Pedro Martinez and Curt Schilling were the other two.

[71] Maddux ended up with 999 walks, Fergie with 997. They retired just in time!

One thing we all remember about Fergie – you had to get to him early, or you were pretty much out of luck. After the third inning, he was pretty much unhittable; at 6 feet 5 inches, he just got stronger and stronger as the game went on.

A Canadian by birth, although many baseball records declare that he was born in 1943, Jenkins maintains that he was born on December 13, 1942. The only Hall of Famer to be born in Canada, he hails from Chatham, Ontario and is the only child of Ferguson Jenkins, Sr. and his wife Delores. The elder Ferguson, a chef, was descended from immigrants from the Bahamas. Delores' ancestors were slaves who escaped the southern United States via the Underground Railroad. His mother was tall at five feet ten inches, and it is not at all surprising that Fergie grew rather tall himself.

Fergie gained a love for sports from his parents who were also good athletes. His mother was an excellent bowler, and his father played semipro baseball with the Black Panthers, an all-black team. Ferguson, Sr. might have competed at the professional level had he played after Jackie Robinson broke the color barrier.

Ferguson played youth baseball in Canada when he was a teenager. His long arms and lanky legs made him a perfect first baseman. He also honed his pitching by practicing in a coal yard. Terry's Coal Yard was located across the street from his house, and Jenkins and his friends used to pick up pieces of coal or rocks and try to hit an ice chute when the rubber flap opened. The exercise involved both accuracy and timing, but wasn't exactly appreciated by the owner of the coal yard, who called Ferguson, Sr. to complain.

So after, they took aim at passing boxcars instead - not to hit them, but to time their throws so their rocks would pass between the cars or enter open boxcars. When a baseball teammate hurt his arm and couldn't pitch, Fergie volunteered to fill in. While he was not dominant that day, Jenkins began to gain confidence in his ability to pitch, buoyed by his hours of rock-throwing practice. Maybe that is what led to his pinpoint control!

During his school years, his natural athletic ability began to emerge. He tried several sports and excelled at most of them. In his years at Chatham Vocational High School, Ferguson chose to compete in track, hockey, and basketball, lettering five times – not baseball? His mother objected to hockey after he got fourteen stitches in his head, so he switched to baseball instead.

Throughout those years, Fergie was encouraged to work on pitching by Gene Dziadura, who had played shortstop in the Cubs' minor league system. Dziadura at that time was a scout for the Philadelphia Phillies and recognized Fergie's raw talent. Their training sessions continued until Jenkins graduated from high school and was signed by the Phillies in 1962.

Fergie's minor league tour took him to Miami, Chattanooga, Buffalo, and Little Rock. In the winter of 1963-64, he played winter ball in Nicaragua. In 1965, he married Anne Katherine (Kathy) Silas and was called up late that season to play for the Phillies. He appeared in seven games, winning two and losing one. On April 21, 1966, after appearing in only one game that season, Jenkins was traded to the Chicago Cubs with Adolfo Phillips and John Herrnstein for Bob Buhl and Larry Jackson. *The Baseball Trade Register* by Joseph L. Reichler lists this trade as the fourth best in Cubs history. (I don't know what the top three were, but they must have been pretty good trades to beat this one!)[72]

Nineteen sixty-seven marked the beginning of Jenkins' best years as a big league pitcher. After spending the previous winter playing in the Dominican Republic and touring with the Harlem Globetrotters, he was chosen for his first All-Star Game. Jenkins was only twenty-four, and struck out six players (Mickey Mantle, Jim Fregosi, Tony Oliva, Harmon Killebrew, Tony Conigliaro, and Rod Carew) in three innings of work. Lacking the ultimate experience of pitching in a World Series, Jenkins believes that performance was one of his

---

[72] Buhl and Jackson were excellent pitchers in their prime but they were pretty much at the end of their careers by this time. Buhl only won six more games in his career, while Jackson won 41.

greatest. Jenkins was selected to the All-Star Game again in '68, '71 (when he led the NL with 24 wins) and '72.

Later that year, he beat the Reds 4-1 for his 20th win in his last start of the 1967 season. That began a streak of six consecutive 20 win seasons, equaling Mordecai Brown's Cub record that had stood for over six decades – and that was in the dead ball era.

Fergie also loved to hit, and he was an excellent hitting pitcher with some home run power. In his first appearance for the Cubs he hit a home run. In 1971, he drove in 20 of his own runs, assuring five or six wins for himself, he estimates. That season Jenkins also hit a career-high seven doubles, one triple, and six home runs. His lifetime batting average was only .165, but he hit 13 home runs.

Jenkins was the ace of the 1969 pitching staff that almost won the National League pennant; Ken Holtzman and Bill Hands were the other key starters. But Fergie's banner year was 1971 when he won the National League Cy Young Award and appeared once again in the All-Star Game. He went 24-13 and had an ERA of 2.77. A significant accomplishment that year was striking out 263 batters while walking only 37. He was always stingy with walks and believed that the pitcher's job was to get the batter out, not walk him.[73]

"I tell youngsters to make the batter do half the work. Throw strikes. If the batter takes them, he'll strike out. If you don't throw strikes and give up a walk, you get angry with yourself, your catcher is disappointed, your manager is mad, and the pitching coach is unhappy. In today's baseball, the guys by far don't throw enough strikes."[74] Not being afraid to throw strikes at Wrigley Field can also lead to a lot of home runs. Fergie is number one on the Cubs all-time

---

[73] I wish that more pitchers today had that attitude. It might help shorten the games.

[74] Not surprisingly, Greg Maddux had the exact same attitude. I was in attendance one time where Maddux threw a complete game for the Braves, 6-1 against the Cubs, and threw exactly 75 pitches with only one or two strikeouts. Masterful!

list for home runs allowed with 271 in 2,673-2/3 innings. But I am guessing that a large percentage of those home runs were solo homers.

The Cubs had great hopes of winning the pennant in the years Jenkins played under Leo Durocher, particularly in 1969. On September 9th of that year, the Cubs experienced what some called a bad omen. They had been hot, but their four-man pitching rotation was burning out. That night, a black cat wandered onto the field when the Cubs and Mets played at Shea Stadium. It walked around Ron Santo, who was on deck. The animal then approached the dugout and reportedly hissed at Leo Durocher. Ferguson lost that game to Tom Seaver, and the Cubs continued to spiral downward. It turned out to be the year of the Miracle Mets.

Fergie made one last All Star appearance for the Cubs in 1972. By that time he had made several appearances on the leader boards. He was the National League leader in starts in 1968, 1969, and 1971. In addition, he led the National League in complete games in 1967, 1970 and 1971 and topped the league in strikeouts in 1969 with 273. During the six-season period from 1967 to 1972 when he won at least 20 games each season, Jenkins was the Major League leader in wins and strikeouts. Defensively, Fergie was superb. In four seasons (1968, 1976, 1981, and 1983) he had no errors.

Seven seasons with the Cubs ended in 1973. Fergie had a poor year and suffered a sore knee and tendonitis in his shoulder. The years of continuous overwork were wearing on him. Rumors swirled, suggesting he was over the hill at age thirty. Then the Cubs traded him to the Texas Rangers the following season. He won a career-high 25 games in 1974 and was voted Comeback Player of the Year – Oops! Cubs were wrong again. Jenkins tied with Catfish Hunter for the most wins in the American League in 1974. He spent two seasons in Texas before being traded to the Boston Red Sox.

His two seasons in Boston were not as good, his record hovering around the .500 mark. In 1978 Jenkins fared better when he returned to the Rangers and posted an 18-8 record. He pitched with Texas for four seasons before returning to the Cubs in 1982. Fergie returned to the bullpen in Chicago before he retired in 1983 after nineteen major league seasons.

Some think of Ferguson Jenkins as baseball's most unlucky pitcher (Ernie Banks is probably baseball's most unlucky hitter.). By that, I mean that he never made the postseason because he never played for a first place team. He joined Boston one year after they reached the World Series. The year after he retired, the Cubs finished in first place. During his career, Fergie lost thirteen starts by the score of 1-0 despite pitching complete games. I call that bad luck!

In 1980 Fergie hit the headlines, but not for something he was proud of. While he admits to occasional drug use at that time - something he regrets - he claims he was innocent when drugs were found in his luggage during a road trip to Toronto. He found the incident humiliating and although the case against him was ultimately dismissed, he says, "It was about two years before (my father) believed me when I told him I didn't do it." Baseball wasn't immediately convinced either. Commissioner Bowie Kuhn suspended Fergie for twenty games, fined him $10,000, and ordered him to take part in Major League Baseball's drug education program.

## Life after Baseball

As he indicated in his autobiography, *The Game Is Easy, Life Is Hard*, Jenkins has endured numerous personal struggles over the years. He was very close to his mother, who was blind and then died of cancer in 1970. Fergie now supports charities for those two ailments. His first marriage ended in divorce. In 1988, he married Mary-Anne Miller, a softball player, and moved to a ranch near Guthrie, Oklahoma. At that time, Fergie was working as pitching coach for the Texas Rangers' Class AAA team. Sadly, Mary-Anne died as the result of an automobile accident. In the fall of 1992 Fergie planned to accept a coaching position with the Cincinnati Reds' farm team in Chattanooga, Tennessee. Tragically, his fiancée committed suicide, taking Ferguson's three-year-old daughter with her. They both died of carbon monoxide poisoning.

"I learned early on that life is fleeting. I buried a mother when she was young, fifty-two. I buried a wife when she was very young, only thirty-two. I buried a daughter when she was only three. I buried a close friend of mine who was in her thirties. I buried my dad who was eighty-nine. In my life I've been a part of many funerals. At one point I told a reporter I should be in a rubber room."

Rather than ending up in an asylum, Ferguson took his grief and turned it into good works. He supports many charities and takes part in numerous charity events in the United States and his native Canada. In 2000 he registered his charity foundation, The Fergie Jenkins Foundation. On a happy personal note, Ferguson married Lydia Farrington in 1993.

In 1987 Ferguson Jenkins was elected into the Canadian Baseball Hall of Fame. Induction into the National Baseball Hall of Fame in Cooperstown, New York came in 1991, and he was named honorary pitching coach for the 1995 National League All-Stars. SABR voted him one of the top 100 baseball players of the twentieth century in 1999, and I heartily agree.

In 1974 Jenkins, then with the Texas Rangers, became the first baseball player to win the Lou Marsh Trophy, an award given annually to Canada's top athlete. He was also named the *Canadian Press* male athlete of the year four times (1967, 1968, 1971, and 1974). In 2011, the Ontario Sports Hall of Fame created the Ferguson Jenkins Heritage Award in his honor to commemorate those one-of-a-kind events or special moments in time that celebrate the long history of sports in Ontario.

On December 17, 1979, he was made a Member of the Order of Canada for being "Canada's best-known major-league baseball player." Governor General Michaëlle Jean officiated at his investiture into the Order, which finally occurred on May 4, 2007: over 27 years after he was so awarded. On May 3, 2009, the Cubs retired jersey number 31 in honor of both Jenkins and Greg Maddux. On December 13, 2010, Canada Post announced that Jenkins would be honored in Canada with his own postage stamp. The stamp was issued in February 2011 to commemorate Black History Month.

Jenkins still leads the Cubs in all-time team pitching records in strikeouts (2,038) and games started (347), and is the fourth pitcher in history to win more than 100 games in each league. The three who accomplished it before him were Cy Young, Jim Bunning, and Gaylord Perry.

Ferguson Jenkins' lifetime record was 284-226; it would have been even better if he had played on better teams. And look at those complete games! He had 267 complete games in his career, and between 1967 and 1975 those totals were 20, 20, 23, 24, 30, 23, 7, 29, and 22. As I said, Fergie typically got stronger as the game progressed. Nowadays, pitchers rarely pitch a complete game, and most of them are looking to the bullpen for help by the fifth inning.

Ferguson Arthur Jenkins is certainly one of the top three Cub pitchers of all time.

## 24 RICK REUSCHEL

Rick Reuschel might just be the best 214-191 pitcher of all time.

That lifetime record simply does not indicate how good a pitcher he was. Called Big Daddy because of his large frame, Rick Reuschel had a deceptive motion that kept batters constantly off balance. I remember Pete Rose saying that he was one of the best pitchers he ever faced, and Pete – like him or not – got over 4,000 hits in his career. He probably knew what he was talking about when it came to hitting off pitchers.

**Big Daddy – Rick Reuschel – 6'4" and 235**

Ricky Eugene Reuschel wasn't a fat man -- just a big man, 6-3 or 6-4 and 235 pounds, and despite his somewhat paunchy appearance, he was a tremendous athlete. Born May 16, 1949 in Quincy, Illinois, he attended Western Illinois University and was drafted in the third round by the Cubs in 1970. Rick was immediately sent to the minor leagues by the Cubs.

He was in the major leagues less than two years later and installed in the Cubs' starting rotation -- but not until after making his major league debut in relief on June 19, 1972, at Wrigley Field against the Giants. Starting for San Francisco that day was, of all people, Steve Stone – who ended up pitching for the Cubs and later working as the television analyst for both the Cubs and White Sox after his playing career was over.

Rick's brother, Paul, also pitched for the Cubs for a couple of years and was another large man at 6'4" and around 235. (Must be that good farm cooking in Illinois.) In fact, Stone pitched for the Cubs when both Reuschels were on the team. Stone was once asked how the clubhouse food spreads were when he played for the Cubs. His quote: "I have no idea. I never had any, because there was always 500 pounds of Reuschels between me and the spread."

Reuschel went a respectable 10-8 with a fine 2.93 ERA in his rookie season, but did not get a single vote in the 1972 NL Rookie of the Year voting. Perhaps it was because he did not make his first appearance until June. The Cubs were, after all, 85-70 that year and finished second in their division.

The following year he began to define the term "workhorse". Fergie Jenkins was only 14-16 and would get traded after that year, and Milt Pappas was in his last season. From 1973 through 1980 his inning totals were: 237, 240.2, 234, 260, 252, 242.2, 239 and 257. He started between 35 and 39 games each year, never missing a start, and his familiar no-overhead-windup rocking motion, and the big number 48 on his back, were easily recognizable to any Cub fan.

Despite his workhorse qualities, he was really no better than a .500 pitcher until 1977, when he and the rest of the Cubs roared out to a 48-33 start and a 8.5 game lead in late June. On July 28, he was sent into the game against the Reds in relief in the thirteenth inning, and his single began the winning rally in the bottom of the 13th. (Rick was a good hitter -- in 1977, for example, he hit .207/.225/.299 with 3 doubles, a triple, a HR and 8 RBI.)

With that win Reuschel was 15-3 with a 2.14 ERA and was the odds-on favorite to win the NL Cy Young Award. But in true Cub fashion, it didn't happen -- the team collapsed and despite pitching reasonably well the rest of the year, Rick wound up 20-10, and finished third in the Cy Young voting behind Steve Carlton and Tommy John (and also 21st in the 1977 NL MVP balloting). It was the only twenty-win season for a Cubs pitcher between Fergie Jenkins' 24-win season in 1971, and Greg Maddux' 20-win season in 1992.

By 1981, the Cubs had fallen to the depths of the National League, and Rick was off to a mediocre 4-7 start (though with a team that was 15-37 at the time, that's not such a bad record!). So, given the pressure to "do something," GM Bob Kennedy shipped him to the Yankees, in exchange for a player to be named later, who turned out to be Doug Bird, and a prospect named Mike Griffin who never panned out[75]. Bird was a marginally useful starting pitcher, and Reuschel went 4-4 for the Yankees in 11 starts, and did wind up pitching for them in both the split-season 1981 division series, and the 1981 World Series.

But all those seasons of 230+ innings eventually caught up with Rick. By mid-1983 the Yankees tired of Rick and released him. It appeared that he might be finished and resigned to a future in dairy farming in Central Illinois.

But dairy farming would have to wait. Dallas Green, partly for nostalgic reasons and partly because he thought the 34-year-old Reuschel had something left, signed him to return to the Cubs. It was a popular signing for Cub fans who always appreciated Reuschel. Rick made it back to the Cubs for four September 1983 starts, going a respectable 1-1, 3.92, and when Fergie Jenkins was released during spring training 1984, Rick had made it back to the Cubs' major league roster.

Unfortunately, he was about the last man on that '84 pitching staff -- he made only 19 appearances, 14 starts, at one point going from August 10 to September 7 without getting into a game. The rust showed -- he finished 5-5, 5.17, and in a decision that many Cub fans blasted Cub management for, was left off the playoff roster in favor

---

[75] 7-15 lifetime and 2-5 in his one year with the Cubs. Typical Cub post 1950 trade. Doing something usually meant something wrong.

of Green's Philadelphia buddy, Dick Ruthven. Reuschel was just the guy who might have been able to stem the Padre tide in game four or five of the 1984 playoffs. But we will never know.

And Rick's mediocre 1984 season performance prompted Green to let Rick leave the Cubs again, via free agency. He signed with the Pirates and had an outstanding 14-8, 2.27 season in '85. After a middling 1986 and a decent start to the 1987 season in Pittsburgh, he was sent to the contending Giants -- after the trading deadline, in a waiver deal - and helped San Francisco to the NL West title. He didn't pitch well in the NLCS -- allowing seven earned runs in ten innings in two starts -- and the Giants lost.

That didn't stop Rick. Seemingly wanting to prove he could pitch forever, he had two of his best seasons at age 39 in 1988 (19-11, 3.12) and at age 40 in 1989 (17-8, 2.94, 8th in Cy Young voting). But his body began to break down in 1990; he made only fifteen starts, and missed almost the entire 1991 season. He tried to come back for one final year in 1992, but it was clear he had nothing left, and decided to retire.

Despite his build, Rick Reuschel was a good athlete, good enough to be used as a pinch hitter or pinch runner on occasion. He could run surprisingly well for his size (logging 4 triples in his career) and he was frequently used as a pinch runner on days he was not pitching. He was also a fair - though awkward-looking - hitter, batting well over .200 several times.

Rick ranks high on most of the Cubs' all-time pitching lists: 6th in innings (2290), 8th in games (358), 2nd in games started (343), 3rd in strikeouts (1367), and 12th in wins (135; he and Fergie Jenkins are the only ones in the top 12 who pitched for the Cubs after 1945). In a 19-year career, Reuschel compiled a record of 214-191 in 557 games (529 starts). He had 102 career complete games and 26 of those were shutouts. He allowed 1330 earned runs and struck out 2015 batters in 3548 innings pitched.

Rick was also an excellent fielding pitcher. Reuschel was a two-time Gold Glove Award winner and a three-time All-Star. He is among the Top 100 winning pitchers of all time, and he won the Hutch Award[76] in 1985, and was also a winner of The Sporting News Comeback Player of the Year Award.

Like Jenkins before him and Maddux after him, Reuschel did not try to strike out every batter he faced. "He is a fairly idiosyncratic pitcher, using speed changes rather than brute force to bend batters to his will, yet he can throw a 90-plus fastball when he must. He is capable of a good seven-strikeout game, yet much prefers a one-pitch grounder to short. He works well with catchers, without ever feeling the need to talk to them. When he pitches, the mound, like his pitching style, is his, and he prefers to be left alone to perform his craft."[77]

For his retirement, Reuschel stayed true to his modest, low-key self, not giving the press a farewell address to close out his career, and he's remained out of the limelight for the past couple decades. He's a regular at Cubs' spring training fantasy camps in Mesa, Arizona, however.

Since retirement Rick and his brother Paul have operated their family's farm in the Quincy area. Rick owes much to baseball, including his wife - he married his onetime teammate Scot Thompson's sister. I assume she enjoys life on the farm.

Rick Reuschel was definitely an outstanding pitcher in his career – those 214 wins say it all. If he had played on better teams during his career, he might well be in Cooperstown.

**Rick Reuschel on the mound for the Cubs**

[76] Honoring perseverance through adversity

[77] From Ray Rotto of the *San Francisco Chronicle*

# 25 RYNE SANDBERG

Ryne Sandberg was a quiet but true professional who exemplified everything you would want in a baseball player throughout his great Chicago Cub career.

Ryne Sandberg was probably the most popular Chicago Cub player during the last 25 years of the 20th century, and with good reason. He was – along with Joe Morgan – the best second baseman in the National League during that time, and a sure-fire Hall of Famer. Among baseball aficionados, Sandberg is widely considered the best second baseman of his era and perhaps the best ever, especially if one combines offense and defense. This is no small compliment, considering a lineup of second sackers that includes baseball legends Rogers Hornsby, Nellie Fox and Rod Carew. But Sandberg deserves the praise.

Ryno was an outstanding offensive performer and even better defensively. Sandberg finished his career with the highest fielding percentage of all time at second base with .989. He had 15 streaks of 30 or more consecutive errorless games.

Born in Spokane, Wash., in 1959, Ryne D. Sandberg was destined for the baseball diamond. Sandberg's parents were watching a New York Yankees game on the same June afternoon that they were trying to agree on a name for their soon-to-arrive fourth child. When New York brought in a young relief pitcher named Ryne Duren[78], they made their choice right then and there.

Ryne Sandberg became an all-state high school baseball, basketball and football star in Spokane. Parade magazine named Sandberg the starting quarterback on its all-America team in his senior year. Before he graduated in 1978, several universities recruited him to throw the pigskin, but Sandberg chose baseball instead. "I knew it would be a lot easier on my body than football," he said. Smart kid!

Sandberg's signing didn't make headlines. The Philadelphia Phillies chose the teen-age infielder in the 20th round and shipped him straight to Helena, Montana for seasoning in the Rookie League, the bottom rung on the baseball ladder. By 1980, Sandberg had worked his way up to Class-AA ball. Sandberg batted .310 for the Reading, Pa., farm club; led the league's shortstops in fielding percentage (.964), assists (386) and double plays (81); and was named to the Eastern League all-star team. The following September he got his first taste of the majors.

Sandberg appeared in 13 games for the Phillies that September at the age of 21 and committed no errors. His lone hit in six at-bats was a single off – naturally - a Cub pitcher, Mike Krukow.

In January 1982, the Cubs and Phillies were working on a trade of Phillies shortstop Larry Bowa to the Cubs for Cub shortstop Ivan DeJesus. It seems the Phillies were unsuccessful in trying to sign Bowa to a long-term contract. However, Cub general manager Dallas Green, a former Phillies manager, wanted a young prospect to go along with the aging Bowa (as it turned out, Bowa would be out of baseball by 1985). Green had largely been responsible for the Phillies drafting Sandberg in 1978, when Green worked in the Phillies front

---

[78] Ryne Duren threw 100 miles an hour with coke bottle glasses. Batters, therefore, were afraid to face him.

office. Years later, Phillies general manager Paul Owens said that he didn't want to trade Sandberg, but Green and the Cubs weren't interested in any of the other five prospects he offered. Owens then went back to his scouts, who told him Sandberg wouldn't be any more than a utility infielder; this, in spite of the fact that Sandberg had hit over .290 in the minors two years in a row.(Sounds like Cub scouts!)

The *Chicago Tribune's* scouting report, "good speed but a light bat," seemed prophetic when the 22-year-old Sandberg managed only one hit in his first 32 trips to the plate. However, he redeemed himself in what was to become true Sandberg style, finishing the 1982 season with a .271 batting average and leading the team in stolen bases (32) and runs scored (103). Despite his offensive production, the single most important event in his rookie season was the defensive switch that moved Sandberg from third to second base on Sept. 4, 1982.

Sandberg's competitive drive and awesome talent propelled him into the spotlight. He had a good but not spectacular year in 1983, batting .261 for the Cubs. However, in 1984, his third season in the majors, Sandberg and the Cubs had a fairy-tale year. He batted a career-high .314, belted 19 home runs, stole 32 bases and led the majors in runs scored with 114. With a 61-game errorless streak, he won his second straight Gold Glove — committing only six errors all season — and earned his first start in an All-Star Game.

It took a June 23, 1984 afternoon for Sandberg to make everyone in baseball remember his name. During a nationally televised game at Wrigley Field with Harry Caray doing the game, Sandberg tied the Cardinals with homers in both the ninth and 10th innings against Bruce Sutter. His 5-for-6 afternoon with seven RBI in a contest the Cubs eventually won 12-11 caused Cards manager Whitey Herzog to say: "One day I thought he was one of the best players in the N.L.. The next day I think he's one of the best players I've ever seen." Since that day, this game has often been called "The Sandberg Game."

Sandberg's heroics with his bat and glove boosted the Cubs into the postseason for the first time since 1945. Of course, they lost in the playoffs to an inferior San Diego Padres team after taking a 2-0 lead in the National League championship series before they lost three straight in San Diego. He was named National League MVP, becoming the first Cub to win the award since Hall-of-Fame shortstop Ernie Banks in 1959 — the year Sandberg was born.

Ryno gave credit for his remarkable 1984 season, and indeed for his entire career, to then-Cub manager Jim Frey. "I didn't feel that I belonged, that I was good enough to play," recalls Sandberg. At the start of the 1984 season, Frey took his insecure second baseman aside and advised him to just relax and start swinging for the fences. "Jim Frey gave me confidence," said Sandberg,. "When I was first called up by the Phillies, I was surrounded by Pete Rose, Mike Schmidt, Larry Bowa, Steve Carlton — I mean, you're talking an All-Star team. I was afraid to go into the locker room. So out of respect, I didn't go around talking."

Always quiet and reserved as a player, Sandberg always let his bat, and his glove, do most of his talking. He hit 30 home runs for the first time in 1989, when the Cubs reached the postseason for the second time in five years. Although the Cubs failed to reach the World Series both times – this time they lost to the San Francisco Giants and Jack Clark - Sandberg batted .385 with six RBI, five doubles and nine runs scored in two N.L. Championship Series.

In 1990, he led the league in runs scored for the second consecutive year (116) and also led the N.L. with 40 home runs (the first time a second baseman had done that since Rogers Hornsby in 1925). And Sandberg, the first player to win a Gold Glove after changing positions, also set the record for most consecutive errorless games at second base (123).

Sandberg had his second straight .300 season in 1993 (and third in four years), but the 1994 season started out slowly for the 34-year-old slugger. He endured a 1-for-28 slump early in the season and by mid-June was hitting .238, some 50 points below his major-league average. No one in the Cubs organization had any inkling that Sandberg planned to quit during the 1994 season, but few expected Sandberg to come back in 1996, either.

But at the end of 1995, when he went to Wrigley Field to see the final series of the year between the Cubs and the Houston Astros, he knew his place was still on the field, not in the stands.

By spring training 1996, Sandberg had signed on again with the Cubs and was back to business as usual. He regained the power stroke that made him one of the greatest slugging second basemen in history: He hit 25 home runs and drove in 92 runs while also remaining one of the great fielders in the history of the position with just six errors in 1,234 innings. At age 37, he played more games and more innings at that age than any other Cub except outfielder Brian McRae.

At the time of his retirement after the 1997 season, he held the all-time record of 123 consecutive errorless games by a second baseman and also had hit more home runs than any second baseman in baseball history.

Ryne Sandberg is the only second baseman in major-league history to claim nine Gold Gloves. He played four entire seasons in which he did not make a single throwing error. His career fielding percentage of .989 is the best mark by a second baseman in major-league history.

Ryno also is among the Cub all-time home run leaders. Sandberg ranks third in Cub annals in runs scored (1,316) and extra-base hits (761); fourth in doubles (403), hits (2,385), games (2,151), at-bats (8,379), total bases (3,786), stolen bases (344) and singles (1,624); fifth in home runs (282); sixth in RBI (1,061); and eighth in walks (761). Not bad for a high school quarterback!

Perhaps Pete Rose summed up Ryne Sandberg the best. "Ryne Sandberg worked harder than any player I've ever seen. A lot of guys with his athletic ability get by on that and have a nice career. Sandberg worked his butt off because he knew it was wrong not to," said Rose.

Regardless of how one feels about Pete Rose, when Charlie Hustle says you worked harder than anyone else he's seen in a half century in the game, that means you're a pretty hard worker. People may not know about Sandberg's drive to be excellent, though, because he was also one who was not particularly gabby with the media. He let his glove, bat, and feet do the talking.

Ryne Sandberg was a 2005 inductee into the Baseball Hall of Fame in Cooperstown, New York with 76.2% of the votes (393 votes) in his third year of eligibility. I'm not sure why he was not selected in his first year of eligibility, but so be it. The normally shy and quiet Sandberg delivered what many traditionalist fans considered a stirring speech at his Hall of Fame induction ceremony in 2005. He thanked the writers who voted for him because it meant that he played the game the way he had been taught it should be played. He spoke several times of respect for the game, and chided a subset of current players who, in his opinion, lacked that respect. Specifically, he spoke of how the game needs more than home run hitters, citing that turning a double-play and laying down a sacrifice bunt are weapons many of today's greats don't value. He also made a strong pitch for induction of his former Cub teammate, Andre Dawson, who was ultimately elected to join the Hall in 2010.

## Life after His Playing Career Was Over

Many Cub fans thought that Sandberg would never return to the game as a manager – he was just too quiet. However, on December 5, 2006, Sandberg was named manager of the Cubs' Class-A Peoria Chiefs team in the Midwest League. In his first season as a manager, riding the bus between towns like Peoria, Springfield, Ft. Wayne, and Quad Cities, he took his team to the Midwest League championship game. In December 2008, Sandberg was promoted to manager of the Cubs' Class Double-A team, the Tennessee Smokies of the Southern League. In December 2009, he was again promoted, to manager of the Triple-A Iowa Cubs. Upon leading Iowa to an 82–62 record, the Pacific Coast League named him its 2010 Manager of the Year.

Sandberg has said that his ideal job would be to manage the Chicago Cubs. Former manager Lou Piniella suggested that Sandberg, as manager of the Cubs' top minor-league affiliate, would be in the mix to replace him when he retired after the 2010 season. However, the position was given to interim manager nice guy baseball lifer Mike Quade – not the greatest decision the Cubs have ever made.

Feeling that he was never going to get serious consideration from the Cubs, on November 15, 2010, Sandberg left the Cubs organization and returned to his original organization as manager of the Phillies' top minor-league affiliate, the Lehigh Valley IronPigs. He led the IronPigs to the League championship series. *Baseball America* named him its 2011 Minor League Manager of the Year.

After the 2012 season, Sandberg was promoted to third base coach and infield instructor of the Philadelphia Phillies. He was promoted to interim manager of the Phillies after they fired Charlie Manuel on August 16, 2013. Sandberg earned his first win as a manager against the Los Angeles Dodgers on Sunday August 18, 2013.

On September 22, 2013 Sandberg was named permanent manager, with a three-year contract, and an option for 2017. He became the first Hall-of-Fame player to manage a team full-time since Frank Robinson managed the Montreal Expos/Washington Nationals from 2002 to 2006. He entered 2015 with an aging team that was among the worst baseball teams in the major leagues. And in June of 2015, Ryno abruptly resigned as manager of the Phillies.

Sandberg and his second wife, Margaret, are active in charity work for kids. He has five children and five grandchildren of his own.

If Ernie Banks was Mr. Cub for the 50's and 60's, Ryne Sandberg was certainly Mr. Cub for the 80's and 90's.

**Manager Ryne Sandberg – Peoria Chiefs**

# 26 MARK GRACE

While Ryne Sandberg was typically quiet and unassuming, Mark Grace was more outgoing and a darling of the media – always a good interview.

Mark Grace was a very good player, though he will probably never receive serious consideration for the baseball Hall of Fame. He just never hit enough home runs – 173 total - at what is traditionally a power position to warrant serious consideration for the HOF.

Still, his statistics were impressive. He led the majors in hits and doubles during the 1990's. He had a lifetime batting average of .303, with an on base percentage of .383. Grace also had 2445 hits, of which 2201 came in a Cub uniform. In fact, his career lasted 16 years – 1988 through 2003 – and the first thirteen were in a Cub uniform.

Of course, his career was somewhat overshadowed by another Chicago first baseman who played at the same time as Grace. Frank Thomas of the White Sox is a Hall of Famer, with career totals of a

.301 batting average, .419 on base percentage, and 521 home runs. While Thomas was an extremely mediocre first baseman, Grace was outstanding defensively.[79] Grace's fielding percentage for his career was .995 and he was a four-time Gold Glove winner. Yet, he was always overshadowed in Chicago by Thomas.

Mark Eugene Grace was born June 28, 1964 in Winston-Salem, North Carolina, the second son of Gene and Sharon Grace. Since the family moved 13 times in 25 years, Mark was forced to learn how to make friends quickly and adapt to new situations. These characteristics were deeply ingrained in his personality, as today Mark is known for his outgoing demeanor and happy-go-lucky manner.. Moving from city to city throughout his childhood removed any trace of shyness he may have had, and instilled in Mark a gregariousness that would make him a crowd favorite on every team he played for.

One of the family's many stops was the city of St. Louis, Missouri. Here, Mark followed the St. Louis Cardinals and idolized the team's All-Star first baseman, Keith Hernandez. Little did he know that years later, baseball analysts would be comparing his skills to those of his idol. In fact, their careers and style of play closely resembled each other's. Both were regarded as smooth fielding defensemen, solid line-drive hitters, and fan favorites.

Mark's high school years were spent in southern California. He attended Tustin High School near Los Angeles, playing on both the varsity baseball and basketball teams. Mark was a popular student and was even a member of the prom court his senior year – not surprising, since he was a pretty good looking guy and well-liked. However, Southern California has always been loaded with high-school athletic talent, and though Mark had an outstanding high-school career, a major college scholarship was not in the cards. Instead, he would take his emerging skills to Saddleback Junior College in Mission Viejo, California beginning in 1983.

---

[79] Thomas, in fact, played much of his career as a designated hitter, with Paul Konerko actually playing first base. I would not call Thomas a butcher at first base, but he was definitely nothing special as a fielder.

During his two seasons at Mission Viejo, Mark refined his hitting and fielding skills to the point of catching the attention of major league scouts. At the end of his sophomore year, Mark was drafted by the Minnesota Twins in the 15th round of the January 1984 draft. In what would later be looked back on as a turning point in his life, Mark declined to sign and instead decided to transfer to San Diego State University for his junior year – good for the Cubs, not so good for the Twins.

At San Diego State, Mark set the All-Western Athletic Conference on fire. He batted .395 and had a .465 on-base percentage. He led the Aztecs team in batting average, runs, hits, total bases, doubles, triples, sacrifice flies, RBIs, and game-winning RBIs. Grace won team awards for Most Valuable Player, Best Defensive Player, and Hitters Award (best offensive player) and was named honorable mention All-Western Athletic Conference, Southern Division. Despite all his accomplishments (You would have thought he would have been a first round pick with those stats), scouts were hesitant to take another chance on a player who had refused to sign the previous year. Mark slipped to the 24th round of the June 1985 amateur draft before being picked by the Cubs. It would prove to be one of Chicago's greatest draft selections of all time.

Mark's first year in the minors cemented his reputation as a prospect with a bright future. With the Cubs' Single A team, the Peoria Chiefs, Mark slugged his way to the Midwest League batting title with a .342 average and tied for the league lead in hits (159). He scored 81 runs and had 15 homers in 126 games.[80] Honors began to stack up for Mark. He was named team MVP and was a mid-season and post-season Midwest League All-Star selection.

The next year, Mark was assigned to the Cubs' Double A team, the Pittsfield Cubs. A step up in the level of competition did nothing to slow Mark's ascent to the majors. His 1987 season saw him lead the Eastern League in RBI's with a club-record 101. His keen batting eye also became apparent as he struck out only 24 times in 513 plate

---

[80] The Chiefs at that time were owned by Pete Vonachen, a good buddy of Cub announcer Harry Caray.

appearances. Grace's season batting average was 333 and he continued to show good power numbers with a .545 slugging percentage. On the field, Mark committed only 6 errors in the 121 games he played at first base. Mark again earned the league's MVP award and was named a league all-star.

Grace was again promoted in 1988 as he was called up to the Cubs' Triple A team in Iowa. His stay in AAA ball was short, however, as the Cubs had Mark on the fast track. Mark played in only 21 games with the Iowa Cubs before he got the call from Chicago that he was headed to Wrigley Field on May 2, 1988. And so, with a little more than 2 years in the minors, Mark was headed to the majors at just under the age of 24.

As soon as he was called up, Grace showed he could play with the major leaguers. Within a few weeks of being called up, the team's coaching staff knew they were looking at the Cubs' first baseman of the future. As a result, the Cubs traded then-starting first baseman Leon Durham to the Cincinnati Reds. And Mark was installed as the Cubs' starting first baseman within three weeks of joining the team.

Mark's rookie season treated the Wrigley faithful to a preview of things to come. Grace batted .296 and played outstanding defense for the Northsiders. He finished second in the National League Rookie of the Year voting to Chris Sabo, although he was voted Rookie of the Year by *The Sporting News*. The Cubs finished in fourth place with a 77-85 record, but with a team nucleus that now featured Grace, Ryne Sandberg, Greg Maddux, Andre Dawson, Rafeal Palmeiro, Rick Sutcliffe, and emerging pitcher Mike Bielecki, along with rookies Jerome Walton and Dwight Smith, things were looking up at the corner of Clark and Addison.

In 1989, Mark and the Cubs created a stir of excitement in Chicago. The team's emerging stars and veteran leadership combined to form a winning chemistry. Mark played a key role in the team's drive to the NL East division title. He hit .314, the first of his many .300 seasons, and committed only 6 errors (and that with the very wild Shawon Dunston throwing to him!). As Cub hysteria grew throughout the city, the "Boys of Zimmer" ran away from the New York Mets to win their division with a 93-69 record, and a matchup against the San Francisco Giants.

The 1989 NLCS will always be remembered for the outstanding performance of two players, both first basemen: Mark Grace and Will Clark of the Giants. Mark was brilliant in the series, going 11 for 17 (.647 average) with 5 extra base hits and 8 RBIs. It was one of the greatest performances in post-season play, yet it was eclipsed by the play of Will Clark. Clark batted 13 for 20 (.650 average) with 6 extra base hits and 8 RBIs. Despite Mark's heroics, the Giants behind Clark's inspired play held off the Cubs for a 4-1 series victory. Although Mark's team failed to capture the NL crown, he certainly captured the hearts of Cub fans everywhere.

Starting in 1990, however, the Cubs started an eight year run of never finishing above 3rd place in their division. Many of the team's stars from the late eighties were traded away (giving rise to the Ex-Cub Factor and many great careers elsewhere – think Greg Maddux!). Mark Grace remained faithful to the team that had drafted him, and throughout this eight year period teamed with Ryne Sandberg and Sammy Sosa, who joined the team in 1992, to be the only bright spots on otherwise forgettable Cubs teams. In 6 of these 8 seasons, Mark batted over .300. He represented the NL in the 1993, 1995 and 1997 All-Star games. He earned Rawling's Gold Glove Awards for his "Graceful" play in the field during the 1992, 1993, 1995 and 1996 campaigns. Mark had perhaps his finest season statistically in 1996, when he lead the NL with 51 doubles, batted .326, hit 16 home runs and drove in 92 RBIs. He finished 13th in NL MVP balloting that year – largely because the Cubs were simply not pennant contenders.

1998, however, was another story for the Cubs. Entering the season, sportswriters predicted the team would once again finish near the bottom of the NL Central Division. Yet the team came together behind the veteran leadership of Mark Grace, Sammy Sosa, and pitcher Kevin Tapani. Mark did his part to help the Cubs reach the postseason, batting .309 for the year and setting a career high with 17 home runs. Although the Houston Astros ran away with the NL Central division, the Cubs battled the San Francisco Giants over the season's final two months for the NL wild card. The teams ended the regular season with identical 89-73 records, which set the stage for a dramatic one game playoff for the right to play the Atlanta Braves in the National League Division Series. The Cubs prevailed in the playoff game, 5-3, with Mark getting two hits and a walk in the game. Unfortunately, the Cubs had a dismal performance against the heavily-favored Atlanta Braves in the NLDS, losing in three straight games.

Mark continued to put up consistent numbers in 1999 and 2000, and it appeared he would become one of those rare players that would play his entire career with one team. Not since Ernie Banks had the Cubs embraced a player with as much admiration as they had Mark. And for his part, Mark made it known that he looked forward to playing out his career with the team and the city that he had come to know and love. Yet injuries in 2000 that limited his playing time, and prospects in the minors, led general manager Andy McPhail – often nicknamed F_A_I_L during his tenure with the Cubs - to not even negotiate with Grace after the 2000 season.

However, Arizona principal owner Jerry Colangelo – a Chicago native and Cub fan before he bought the Diamondbacks - recognized the leadership Mark could provide both on and off the field and signed him to a two year contract days after his release by the Cubs. "Arizona called me up, and I was a Diamondback about two minutes later," Mark explained. "That's where I always enjoyed playing, and I knew a lot of guys on the team and knew what that organization was all about. Jerry is a guy that any player would love to play for."

Mark joined a 2001 Diamondbacks' lineup that featured ex-teammates Luis Gonzalez, Miguel Batista and Mike Morgan, as well as veterans Matt Williams, Steve Finley, Jay Bell, Tony Womak, Curt Schilling and Randy Johnson. The team was definitely built to win immediately, especially with Johnson and Schilling as its 1-2 starters. Grace returned to form offensively and batted .298 on the season with 15 home runs, including a round-tripper in his first game at Bank One Ballpark.

The Diamondbacks won the National League pennant and faced the mighty New York Yankees in the World Series. The 2001 World

Series will go down as one of the most memorable Fall Classics in history. Mark would play a special part in the series. In the first World Series appearance of his career, Mark hit a double and drove in two runs in Game 1. He would hit a mammoth upper deck home run in Game 5 off Yankee reliever Orlando Hernandez. But Mark saved his best performance for Game 7, hitting safely twice before, in the most important at bat of his career, leading off the now legendary 9th inning rally with a single up the middle that would set the stage for Luis Gonzalez's game-winning hit later in the inning.

Mark Grace, would go on to finish his career with the Diamondbacks, playing two additional seasons in the desert. Yet age was catching up to him, and his batting average and fielding skill began to diminish over this period. In 2002, Mark was still the Diamondbacks' starting first baseman. But by 2003, he had been relegated to a pinch hitter and mentor to young first base prospect Lyle Overbay. With his batting average at .200, Grace decided to call it quits after the 2003 season.

## Life after His Playing Career Was Over

After retiring, Grace was immediately hired by the Diamondbacks as their color commentator. He was paired with Thom Brennaman on television from 2004 to 2006 and with Daron Sutton from 2007 to 2012. However, alcohol and drunk driving problems ended his broadcasting career. On August 24, 2012 Grace requested an indefinite leave of absence from the booth, and at the end of the 2012 season, the team announced that he would not be returning for the 2013 season. He was sentenced to four months in prison in 2013 for driving while intoxicated.

Grace then served as a minor league hitting instructor for the Diamondbacks in 2013 and 2014. In February 2015, he joined the parent team as assistant hitting coach.

Mark finished his career with a lifetime .303 batting average, 2445 hits, a .995 fielding percentage, and four gold glove awards. Yet he gave to the game more than statistics. His love of the game and old-school approach won over legions of fans in both Chicago and Arizona, and he remains a popular figure in both cities.

Perhaps the *Chicago Tribune* put it best with this quote on Grace's retirement in 2003. "For 16 seasons, Mark Grace brought enthusiasm, humor and amazing talent to the game of baseball. As a Chicago Cub, Mark led his team on the field and in the hearts of its fans from his rookie season in 1988 through the end of the 2000 season. His thirteen seasons playing for the Cubs established him as one of the game's 'good guys' with a throwback style of getting his uniform dirty and having fun on and off the field."

Perhaps that is why he was nicknamed "Amazing Grace."

**Mark Grace celebrating Cub wild card playoff win in 1998 – a rare sight to be sure.**

# APPENDIX – LOU BROCK FOR ERNIE BROGLIO TRADE

Many times during the course of this book, I have referred to the infamous Lou Brock for Ernie Broglio trade and called it the worst trade in the history of the Cubs. According to my research the phrase "Brock for Broglio" is sometimes used in the sport of baseball to signify a trade that in hindsight, turns out to be an extremely lopsided transaction.

Those two players were the centerpieces of a June 15, 1964, six-player deal: Brock, Jack Spring and Paul Toth were traded from the Chicago Cubs to the St. Louis Cardinals in exchange for Broglio, Bobby Shantz, and Doug Clemens.

It was thought initially the Cubs had done better in the deal, as Broglio was coming off some impressive seasons while pitching for the Cardinals, while Brock had been considered a disappointment for the Cubs.

Almost immediately the effects of the trade were felt, as Brock would bat .348 for the Cardinals and lead them to winning the 1964 World Series. (He was basically a .250 hitter in his 2+ seasons with the Cubs.) Brock also helped the Cardinals to another World Series title in 1967, a pennant in 1968, and played successfully for St. Louis through 1979, amassing 3,023 hits and 938 stolen bases (at the time becoming baseball's all-time leader in stolen bases) en route to his Hall of Fame election in 1985. Meanwhile, Broglio went only 4-7 with a 4.04 ERA for the Cubs – that is for the rest of his career, by the way, not just the 1964 season, and by 1966 was out of Major League Baseball. Broglio did not tell anyone at the time, but he was suffering from an injured elbow since the second-half of the 1963 season, and in November 1964, had his ulnar nerve reset. Didn't the Cubs have medical staff examine him before the trade?

This is sometimes referred to as the most lopsided trade in baseball history. I can't think of a worse one.

**Lou Brock in the process of stealing yet another base**

**Ernie Broglio – in his Chicago Cub uniform – unfortunately for Cub fans.**

I wish to acknowledge the following references used in this book:

1. www.jackbales.com
2. www.19cbaseball.com
3. Society for American Baseball Research – www.sabr.com – various writers.
4. www.capanson.com
5. http://www.thenationalpastimemuseum.com/article/bill-lange-star-wrong-profession and information provided by Gabriel Schechter
6. http://fromdeeprightfield.com/
7. www.neatorama.com
8. www.bleedcubbieblue.com
9. www.baseball-reference.com
10. www.sportsonearth.com – article by Phil Rogers on Ernie Banks
11. www.markgrace.com
12. Wrigley Field photo provided by contemporary romance novelist Julie James
13. Book front and back covers designed by Larry Puhl

# ABOUT THE AUTHOR

Gary Koca has had a love of baseball for as far back as he can remember. Professionally, he worked in human resources for 42 years, either as a Federal government employee or contractor. He has written hundreds of position papers, proposals, articles for journals, letters, and many other written products during that time. Now retired and able to devote more time to writing about his two favorite topics – baseball and old movies from the 1930's, 40's, and 50's - his major character flaw is being a life-long fan of the Chicago Cubs. Gary is married with two daughters and four grandchildren and lives in suburban Chicago.

Made in the USA
Middletown, DE
05 September 2016